Modularisation of Vocational Education in Europe

NVQs and GNVQs as a model for the reform of initial training provisions in Germany?

Modularisation of Vocational Education in Europe

NVQs and GNVQs as a model for the reform of initial training provisions in Germany?

HUBERT ERTL

Monographs in International Education
Series Editors: Colin Brock & Rosarii Griffin

Symposium Books
PO Box 65 Wallingford, Oxford OX10 0YG, United Kingdom
www.symposium-books.co.uk

Published in the United Kingdom, 2000

ISBN 1 873927 98 3

Typeset in Melior by Symposium Books
Printed and bound in the United Kingdom by Biddles Ltd *www.biddles.co.uk*

Contents

List of Acronyms and Abbreviations

A level	Advanced Level of the GCE examination
APL	Accreditation of prior learning
AS level	Advanced Supplementary level of the GCE examination
BTEC	Business and Technology Education Council
CAT	Credit Accumulation and Transfer
CBET	Competency-based Education and Training
CEDEFOP	European Centre for the Development of Vocational Training (Centre Européen pour la Développement de la Formation Professionnelle)
C & G	City and Guilds of London Institute
COMETT	European Community Action Programme in Education and Training for Technology (programme on cooperation between universities and enterprises in the field of technology)
CPVE	Certificate of Pre-vocational Education
DfE	Department for Education
DfEE	Department for Education and Employment
ECU	European Currency Unit
ED	Employment Department
EDEXCEL	Educational Excellence
EDPM	European Dimension Pedagogical Material
EEC	European Economic Community
ERASMUS	European Community Action Scheme for the Mobility of University Students
ETUCE	European Trade Union Committee for Education
EU	European Union
EURATOM	European Atomic Energy Committee
EUROFORM	European Community Framework for New Skills and New Employment Opportunities Induced by Technological Change and the Single Market
EUROTECNET	European Technology Network for Training (European Community Action Programme for the Promotion of Innovation in Vocational Training resulting from Technological Change)
FESC	Further Education Staff College

FEU	Further Education Unit
FORCE	Action Programme for the Development of Continuing Vocational Training in the European Community (Formation Continue en Europe)
GCE	General Certificate of Education
GCSE	General Certificate of Secondary Education
GNVQ	General National Vocational Qualification
GSVQ	General Scottish Vocational Qualification
HMI	Her Majesty's Inspectorate
ILO	International Labour Organisation
IRIS	European Community Network of Training Programmes for Women
LEONARDO DA VINCI	European Community Action Programme on Vocational Training
LINGUA	Programme for the Promotion of Foreign Language Knowledge in the European Community
MES	Modules of Employable Skills
MSC	Manpower Services Commission
NC	National Certificate
NCVQ	National Council for Vocational Qualifications
NRA	National Record of Achievement
NVQ	National Vocational Qualification
OFSTED	Office for Standards in Education
QCA	Qualifications and Curriculum Authority
PETRA	European Community Action Programme for the Vocational Training of Young People and Their Preparation for Adult and Working Life
RSA	Royal Society of Arts
SCAA	School Curriculum and Assessment Authority
SCOTVEC	Scottish Vocational Education Council
SEA	Single European Act
SEDOC	Register of Occupations and Professions in International Exchange
SEM	Single European Market
SOCRATES	European Community Action Programme on Education
SVQ	Scottish Vocational Qualification
TEC	Training and Enterprise Council
TQM	Total Quality Management
TVEI	Technical and Vocational Initiative
VET	Vocational Education and Training
YT	Youth Training
YTS	Youth Training Scheme

Glossary of German Terms

Allgemeine Preußische Gewerbeordnung	Prussian Trade and Industry Code
Anerkannte Ausbildungsberufe	Recognised training occupations
Abitur	Leaving certificate from the Gymnasium; usually confers eligibility for higher education entrance
Ausbildung	Training
Ausbildungsordnung	Training regulation
Ausbildungsrahmenplan	Overall training plan
Berufliche Handlungsfähigkeit	Ability of the individual to act and work competently in an occupational/vocational environment
Berufsbild	Occupational profile
Berufsbildposition	Element of occupational profile
Berufsbildungsgesetz (BBIG)	Vocational Training Act
Berufsbildungspaß	'Passport of vocational education'
Berufsfachlicher Arbeitsmarkt	Vocationally oriented labour market
Berufskonzept	'Concept of the vocation'
Berufsschule	Vocational school
Bundesministerium für Bildung, Wissenschaft, Forschung und Technologie (BMBF)	Federal Ministry of Education, Science, Research and Technology
Bundesinstitut für Berufsbildung (BIBB)	Federal Institute for Vocational Training
Deutsche Industrie Norm	German Industrial Standard
Deutscher Ausschuß für das Technische Schulwesen (DATSCH)	German Committee of Technical Education

EurowirtschaftsassistentIn (EUWAS)	Pilot project for the training of assistants in European business administration
Facharbeiterbrief	Certificate of completed apprenticeship
Fachhochschule	Specialised institution of higher education (polytechnic)
Fortbildungsschule	Further training school
Gesellenbrief	Certificate of completed apprenticeship
Gewerbeordnung des Norddeutschen Bundes	Trade and Industry Code of the North German Confederation
Gymnasium	General education secondary school providing general university entrance qualification
Großer Befähigungsnachweis	Comprehensive certificate of competence
Handwerksordnung	Crafts Code
Hochschulreife	University entrance certificate
Kleiner Befähigungsnachweis	Limited certificate of competence
Kollegschule	College school
Kultusministerkonferenz (KMK)	Conference of Land Ministers of Education and Cultural Affairs
Land, Länder	Federal State, Federal States
Qualifizierungspaß	'Qualification passport'
Rahmenlehrplan	Skeleton curriculum
Zentralverband des Deutschen Handwerks (ZDH)	Central Association of German Handicrafts
Zuständige Stellen	Competent Bodies

CHAPTER 1

Introduction

Modularisation in vocational education and training (VET) provides matter for intense debate in Germany. The effects of this debate may be best illustrated by the decisively differing opinions within the Federal Institute for Vocational Training (*Bundesinstitut für Berufsbildung – BIBB*), sometimes referred to as the 'Parliament of VET', comprising the representatives of employers and trade unions as well as the federal and state governments. At its meeting in March 1997, the *BIBB* General Committee was not able to pass a declaration of principle concerning the future development of the Dual System of VET because an agreement on the question of modularisation could not be reached. Although there was agreement on all other major questions of initial and further training, the disagreement of employers and trade unions about modular structures could not be bridged (Kloas, 1997a, p. 18; Pütz, 1997, p. 67).

The major focus of the debate about modularisation in Germany, and in the European Union (EU), seems to be driven by educational policy rather than by arguments concerning pedagogical aspects or the teaching/learning process (Münk, 1995, p. 35ff.; Pütz, 1997, p. 63). The arguments put forward by supporters of modularisation seem to be unclear and sometimes dubious [1]; on the other hand, the opponents of modular structures simply put forward the 'concept of the vocation', which determines the main characteristics of VET in Germany and which is enshrined in law, and describe it as incompatible with any type of modularisation.[2] Both positions seem to be inappropriate starting points for a serious and unbiased analysis of the potential advantages modularisation has to offer for the German VET system. Because of this lack of consensus or the wholesale rejection of modularisation, it can be found only in comparatively small areas of VET, e.g. the qualification of specific target groups, further training and schemes for additional qualifications in initial training (Davids, 1996; Kloas, 1996; Reuling & Sauter, 1996, p. 6; Zedler, 1996, p. 20; Sloane, 1997a, p. 224).

As a member of the EU, there is an increasing pressure on training provisions in Germany, resulting from the ongoing process of economic integration and the competition that now exists between vocational training systems of the member states resulting from the mobility of labour within the EU. Commentators regard the Dual System of training as being potentially endangered by these European challenges if it is not reformed in the near future (Münk, 1997, p. 6ff.) Other commentators emphasise the rapid globalisation and changing industrial relations within and between countries as the main sources for reform pressure on the German training system (Kutscha, 1998, pp. 274–282). Irrespective of where the need for reform has arisen, modularisation of vocational education is one of the major proposals for such a reform process.

Against this background, this study aims to investigate the possibilities of modularisation in the German initial training sector. It is my opinion that the discussion about modularisation in German VET must take the developments in other European countries into account. In particular, the EU as an institution as well as a concept will increasingly determine broad areas of the societal development in its member states. Therefore, the strategies for the creation of modular structures in the German training system cannot develop in isolation from the approaches towards modularity in other European countries. With regard to the search for possible models for reform in Germany, the National Vocational Qualification (NVQ) framework in England and Wales seems particularly interesting. Unlike the approaches in Spain, France and the Netherlands, which are also briefly illustrated in this study, the NVQ model has been created to reform an entire existing training system. This task is comparable to the role modularisation would play if used as a modernisation strategy for German provisions.

Chapter 2 provides an overview of vocational training in Germany at present. The emphasis lies on the Dual System as the main sector in which young people in Germany attain their initial vocational qualification. The 'concept of the vocation' as the underlying principle of the Dual System and its influence on the debate about the modernisation of the training sector are examined and form the basis for a conceptualisation of modularisation in the next chapter.

The detrimental effects of the unclear and ambiguous use of the terms 'module' and 'modularisation' on the debate in Germany are widely acknowledged (e.g. Wiegand, 1996a, p. 261ff.) Therefore, an attempt is made to clarify and conceptualise the relevant terminology in chapter 3. As a result, three concepts of modular structures are presented which are discussed in the German context. All examples of modularisation given in this study will be described in terms of the concepts derived in chapter 3.

Stimulated by the provisions of the EU in the field of vocational education and training and educational systems in other countries, the debate in Germany about modularisation seems to be gathering pace (Cleve, 1995, p. 12). The provisions of the EU as they unfold today, the influence of the EU on its member states' systems of VET, and the different approaches of European countries towards modularisation will be illustrated in chapter 4. As to the wider implications of 'European modules' in VET, their potential to enhance the European dimension in education is examined.

The highly modularised NVQ model in England and Wales is regularly held up as an example for a European reference system of vocational qualifications for the future (Wiegand, 1996a, p. 271). The ideas behind the NVQ model, its structure and its formation of vocational qualifications, most prominently NVQs and GNVQs, are discussed in some detail in chapter 5.[3]

In conclusion, chapter 6 proposes a strategy for modularisation in the German initial training sector. It suggests the evolution of existing elements of occupational profiles into modules, as outlined in chapter 3. The strategy is developed on the basis of the conclusions from previous chapters and draws mainly on the experiences of NVQs and GNVQs in England and Wales. The European perspective is important in so far as the modular approaches and good practice in EU member states can provide a valuable knowledge base for the German context. The strategy is rooted in the existing legislative framework as described in chapter 2, as there seems to be a strong consensus across all social groups that the 'concept of the vocation' must not be endangered by modernisation developments of any kind. Suggestions are made for further debate about the proposal itself and the necessary changes to the current assessment and accreditation structures which follow from it.

The appendices provide additional materials to illustrate specific aspects of some of the issues discussed in the main text. The relevant appendices are referred to in the individual chapters.

The comparative elements of this study are informed by the conviction that the systems of education and training are deeply embedded in the cultural environments and traditions of the society they have developed in. Therefore, it is not possible to take over arbitrarily selected parts of an educational practice from a foreign system to improve the domestic one. Michael Sadler (1900, p. 49) has outlined this abuse of comparative education in a frequently quoted illustration:

> *We cannot wander at pleasure among the educational systems of the world, like a child strolling through a garden and pick off a flower from one bush and some leaves from another, and then expect that if we stick what we have gathered into the soil at home, we shall have a living plant.*

Nevertheless, the study attempts to make best use of the property of the comparative approach in that it 'enlarges the framework within which we can view the results obtained in a single country: by providing counterinstances, it challenges us to refine our theories and test their validity against the reality of different societies' (Noah, 1984, p. 558). This critical aspect of the comparative approach seems to be particularly valuable for the development of a modular strategy in German VET.

CHAPTER 2

Vocational Education and Training in Germany

The Tradition of Vocational Training [4]

As in other countries, the original form of vocational training in Germany, dating back to the Middle Ages, was the master craftsman training his apprentice.[5] Throughout the Middle Ages, apprenticeship training was widespread and subject to the strict control of the guilds. By the sixteenth century, however, the guilds and the apprenticeship system had degenerated into a deplorable state. Training of apprentices declined into mere exploitation of young people due to the disappearance of the guilds' regulating powers.

Legislative initiatives throughout the nineteenth century (the Prussian Trade and Industry Code [*Allgemeine Preußische Gewerbeordnung*] of 1845 [amended in 1897] and, more importantly, the Trade and Industry Code of the North German Federation [*Gewerbeordnung des Norddeutschen Bundes*] of 1869) can be regarded as attempts to fill the vacuum left by the loss of the guilds' powers (Deissinger, 1996b, p. 318ff.) Nevertheless, it was not until 1908 that the 'limited certificate of competence' (*Kleiner Befähigungsnachweis*) [6] was introduced and stabilised the provisions satisfactorily: under this amendment of the Trade Code, an employer wishing to provide training had to furnish proof of his qualifications as a master craftsman. From the last third of the nineteenth century onwards, industry and commerce increasingly based their vocational training on the model of the craftsman apprenticeship.[7] Consequently, the industry-led 'German Committee of Technical Education' (*Deutscher Ausschuß für das Technische Schulwesen – DATSCH*) established industry-specific training structures incorporating the 'concept of the vocation', which also underpins the apprenticeship system as developed within the crafts (Benner, 1997a, p. 56ff.)

Within the crafts and industry, the rise of natural sciences and modern technologies made it increasingly necessary to have a theoretical foundation upon which to base practical work. As theory could no longer be learned solely through experience, classes had to be held to remedy any deficits in basic education and to supplement practical training. From the beginning of the nineteenth century onwards, this role was assumed by further training schools (*Fortbildungsschulen*), which often originated from religious Sunday schools which were mostly founded in the eighteenth century. Alongside the industrial Sunday schools, whose ethos drew on the ideas of the Enlightenment and mercantilism, religious Sunday schools gradually assumed the role of teaching the theoretical foundations relating to apprentices' occupations.[8] The Trade and Industry Code of 1869 underlined the generally recognised importance of these further training schools.

It is important to note that the stabilisation of the craft apprenticeship system, the development of training provisions in the industrial sector, and the expansion of further training schools all took place fairly independently of each other, despite happening at approximately the same time (Greinert, 1994, p. 22). It was not until the turn of the century that attempts were made to amalgamate these different sectors into a special form of qualification, a form that became known as the Dual System of vocational education.

From the first half of the twentieth century onwards, this new system survived the upheavals caused by the Great Depression and the two World Wars. Furthermore, it was not substantially altered by the emerging models of industrial apprentice training, but integrated these new models into the framework that was established by craft and industry at around the turn of the century. Also, from 1900 onwards, the further training schools lost their original role of remedying the lack of basic education, as the elementary school sector was substantially expanded (Groothoff, 1964, p. 20). Consequently, they shifted their pedagogic emphasis to that of supplementing vocational training in enterprises and as a result, the development of vocational schools (*Berufsschulen*) in the contemporary sense had begun.[9] The term *Berufsschule* was applied to those institutions in 1920, and by 1938 attendance had become compulsory (Her Majesty's Inspectorate [HMI], 1995, p. 17).

After the Second World War, the Dual System was met with general approval but it was not until the 1969 Vocational Training Act (*Berufsbildungsgesetz – BBIG*) that the various strands of vocational training legislation were brought together and that the basis for a large-scale rationalisation was provided.[10] The apprenticeship system was extended to sectors other than the crafts and various industries. The Act also clarified the role of the state. The system may be best described as a *state-controlled market model* [11] in which the state sets the guidelines for the cooperation of employers and trade unions.[12] This model is regarded as an efficient way of limiting the risks of 'market failure' on the one hand and 'state failure' on the other (Kutscha, 1995, p. 10). Furthermore, the Act reduced the number of recognised training occupations and the training regulations for these occupations were updated. With the unification of the two German states in 1990, this regulative framework became effective in the new federal *Länder*.[13] Measures implemented from the mid-1980s to the early 1990s in order to restructure certain areas of the system did not change its fundamental form. Most importantly, change took place on a micro- rather than a macro-didactic level (see next section and appendix I).

Germany's system of VET can be explained largely by this distinctive tradition. The dominance of the Dual System of training is only one illustration of the fact that today's provisions must be seen as the 'updated past' and that they do not exist in isolation from processes which existed in the past (Deissinger, 1994, p. 32). The development of the Dual System in this century may be divided into four major phases (Table I).

Pre-Phase: Middle Ages–late nineteenth century
Development and decline of guild-controlled craft apprenticeships.
Foundation of religious and industrial Sunday schools.

Foundation Era: 1870–1920
Restoration of craft apprenticeships and further training schools based on the Trade and Industry Code of 1869.

Consolidation Phase: 1920–70
Development of industry-specific apprenticeships and integration into the existing training system. The term *Berufsschule* becomes accepted and attendance is compulsory from 1938.

Expansion Phase: starting in 1970
Government influence and rationalisation based on the Vocational Training Act of 1969, effective in the new federal *Länder* from 1990.

Table I. Stages of development of the Dual System in German VET.[14]

The Dual System

In 1964, the German Commission for Education passed a Report on Vocational Training and Education and coined the term 'Dual' for the 'system of simultaneous training in an enterprise and at a vocational school' (cited in Kutscha, 1996, p. 10). This system has attracted the interest of foreign observers for decades, a fact that is primarily due to the constantly high participation rates: a stable 65–70% of school leavers at 16 enter training through the Dual System.[15] A further success of the system is the comparatively smooth transition of young people finishing initial training to continuous employment. This 'second threshold' [16] causes high youth unemployment in many European countries, but in Germany, the high proportion of trainees staying in work after training in the Dual System eases this problem (HMI, 1991, p. 9ff.; Benner, 1992, p. 3). There is already an enormous amount of literature describing the structures, principles and outcomes of the system as a result of the international interest and arising from the research.[17] In this study therefore, it will suffice to give a very brief outline of some of the main characteristics of the Dual System.

Legal Foundation

The main legal basis of VET under the Dual System is the Vocational Training Act (*Berufsbildungsgesetz – BBIG*) of 1969. When the Act was passed, the Crafts Code (*Handwerksordnung*), which deals with training in the craft trades, was modified and adapted in line with the *BBIG*. Thus, we can speak of standardised provisions for all areas of training.[18]

Under the terms of the *BBIG*, employers and trainees commit to a legally binding contract for training in one of about 370 recognised training occupations (*anerkannte Ausbildungsberufe*). The training lasts between 2 and 3½ years (para. 25, 29, *BBIG*) depending on the occupation being followed and the entry qualifications of the trainees.

Venues of Training

Trainees spend about 3 days a week on in-company training and up to 2 days in vocational schools. Whereas federal law (e.g. training regulations – *Ausbildungsordnungen*) regulates the former, the latter falls under the legislation of the *Länder* (e.g. skeleton curricula – *Rahmenlehrpläne*). Harmonisation processes are in place to integrate both parts of the training and to ensure comparability of the provisions in the 16 *Länder*. The term 'Dual' refers primarily to the division of training into two separate training environments, each regulated by its own distinct legislators.[19]

Role of the Chambers

The local, self-governing Chambers of Industry and Commerce, the Crafts Chambers, the Chambers of Agriculture and the Associations of Professions have the status of 'competent bodies' (*zuständige Stellen*) and play a crucial role in the organisation, administration and examination of vocational training. As intermediate organisations between state and companies, they put training laws and regulations into practice.

Following the 'principle of voluntariness', no employer is obliged to take on trainees. However, all firms have to register with a Chamber and those wishing to provide training must be approved by the Chamber as a 'training company'. The approval depends on the equipment and resources of the company, and the qualifications and experience of the trainers working for the company.[20] Furthermore, the local Chamber supervises the organisation and assessment of intermediate and final examinations and acts as an awarding body for vocational qualifications.

Corporative Structures

Typically, supervising and examining bodies set up by the Chambers consist of equal numbers of employers' representatives, employees' representatives and vocational school teachers. The most important of these bodies are the vocational training committee and the board of examiners.

The list of recognised occupations and all related regulations (duration of training, standards, curricula, etc.) are developed and maintained by the Federal Institute for Vocational Training (*Bundesinstitut für Berufsbildung – BIBB*) [21], a body consisting of an equal number of representatives of employers, employees and the federal and *Länder* governments in all its major committees. Decisions are taken with mutual consultation of all groups involved. This 'principle of consensus' is regarded as an expression of a living democracy and of a high commitment to training within society (Schmidt, 1996a, p. 2).[22] However, it is also the reason for time-consuming negotiations whenever the regulations for a recognised occupation are updated.[23]

Assessment and Qualifications

Trainees are assessed for their vocational certificate solely through the intermediate and final examinations. Assessment of coursework normally only counts towards the vocational school certificate, which is of minor importance for the trainee's further career. Those trainees successful in the examinations receive a certificate to indicate their status as skilled workers (*Facharbeiterbrief* or *Gesellenbrief*). This qualification is part of a clear and well-accepted path of advancement within the educational system that gives access either to higher education or to progress and promotion at work.

Cost

Companies provide vocational training at their own expense, and trainees have to be paid an appropriate training wage. The *Land* authorities bear the costs of in-school training. Thus, the total costs of training are shared in the ratio of approximately 40% (*Länder*) and 60% (employers) (Noah & Eckstein, 1988, p. 61).

In the past, many firms trained more young people than they required, but with the recession of recent years, there have been reductions in training as a consequence of cost-cutting measures in firms. Nevertheless, there is still a sense of social responsibility motivating employers to take on trainees (Kutscha, 1995, p. 7).

Vocational Schools

In most *Länder*, vocational schools are organised in five groups of vocational fields, namely: industry, commerce, home economics, agriculture and miscellaneous occupations. Classes are organised according to individual occupations or groups of occupations. The *Berufsschule* provides general and vocational education in order to deepen and supplement on-the-job training.

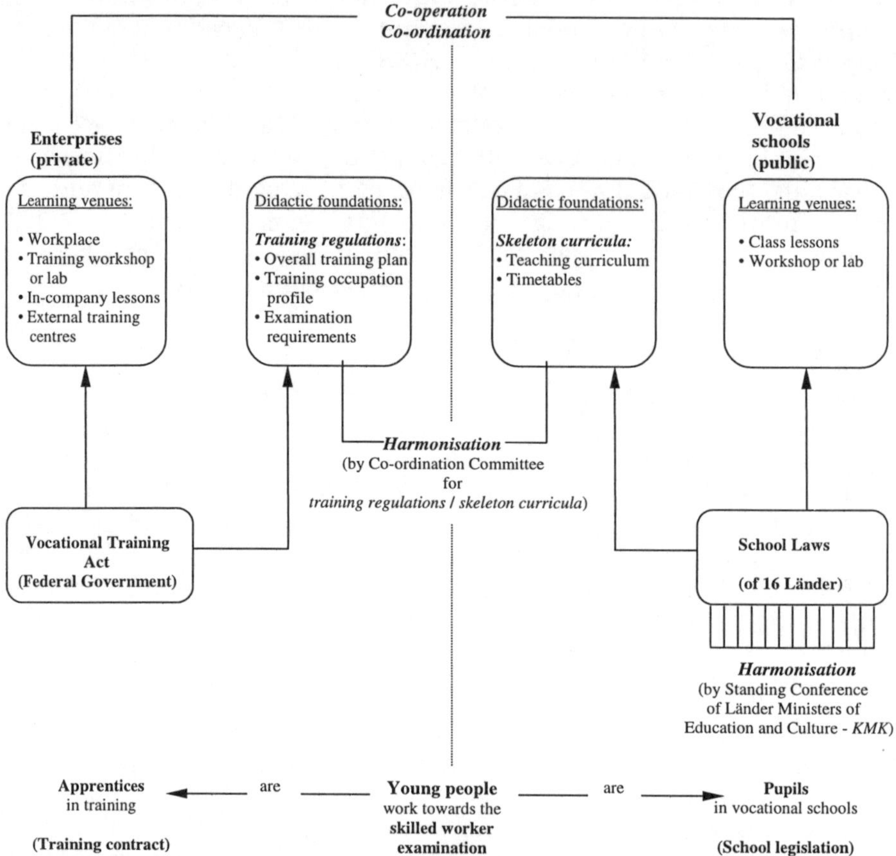

Figure 1. Overview of the structural features of the Dual System.[24]

On average, vocational tuition makes up about 60% of the courses, general education about 40%. The comparatively high proportion of the course contents devoted to extending the trainees' general education is regarded as an essential component within the aims of the 'concept of the vocation', discussed in the next section. Figure 1 sets out the structural connections between the main actors and institutions within the duality of the system.

The 'Concept of the Vocation'[25]

The German 'concept of the vocation' (*deutsches Berufskonzept*) not only lies at the basis of training in the Dual System but also underpins the multitude of leitmotifs and acts of legislation regulating the differentiated system of initial and further qualification in Germany (Benner, 1996, p. 3ff.)[26] For this study, it seems to be sufficient to concentrate on those aspects of the concept that are concerned with the individual's capability to work and act competently in a vocational environment (*berufliche Handlungsfähigkeit*). This capability is regarded as a necessary precondition for any employment and it goes beyond the mere earning of the individual's living, also emphasising the notion of personal development.

The 'concept of the vocation' and underlying social standards are reflected in the Vocational Training Act (*BBIG*) of 1969 and other training regulations. For instance, para. 1(2) of the *BBIG* prescribes a broad basis of vocational education, a well-ordered course of training and the acquisition of sufficient vocational experience for training in one of about 370 state-recognised training occupations (cf. Kuda, 1996, p. 17). These training occupations have an 'exclusive status': young people under the age of 18 are only allowed to be trained in one of the recognised occupations (para. 28(1,2), *BBIG*).[27]

Typically, recognised occupations include the training for the wide range of tasks a skilled worker in a specific field would require. The variety of skill is set out in corresponding occupational profiles (*Berufsbilder*) for each occupation. These profiles are structured into a number of elements (*Berufsbildpositionen*) which are designed to cover the necessary skills and knowledge to fulfil all tasks in a vocation.[28] The profiles are not specific to one company or to one specific task; the 370 training occupations are designed to prepare for about 30,000 specific jobs in companies (Benner, 1997a, p. 54). The qualification should be applicable in many employment contexts and responsive to the changing economic and social environments of a company (para. 25[1], *BBIG*). Skills and knowledge are acquired in dealing with 'real-life' tasks in a company; off-the-job training and general education in vocational schools are intended to supplement and broaden the learning processes of on-the-job training. Moreover, the qualification forms the basis for further training and lifelong learning.[29]

To fulfil these functions, educationists regularly emphasise the importance of so-called 'key qualifications' or 'generic skills'. Mertens (1974) introduced these skills as a pedagogic concept to the educational discussion in Germany in the 1970s. Since then, the concept has provoked controversial debates about the best way of operationalising vague concepts, such as the ability to plan, execute and control occupational tasks independently, the capability to work and assume responsibility in a team, the ability to acquire special skills quickly and to solve problems creatively, and the capacity for abstract and theoretical thought.[30] Despite controversies about the concept, its central idea of enhancing trainees' personal development in order to enable them to fulfil increasingly complex work roles has found its way into the design and updating process of recognised occupations. An illustration of the way in which these ideas influenced the new micro-didactic structure of in-company training is given in appendix I.

Furthermore, the attainment of a skilled worker qualification within a recognised occupation and subsequent employment in a related vocational sector are the basis for classification in the wage system (e.g. minimum wages and salaries) and for measures of social security (e. g. unemployment benefit) in Germany. Sociological studies have concluded that a person is almost exclusively perceived in relation to her/his vocation and that their vocation is used as the main source of information to form an impression of a person (Kell, 1991, p. 300; Bruijn & Howieson, 1995, p. 91ff.; Geissler & Orthey, 1998). Therefore, their vocation is a determining factor for a person's status and identity.

The categorisation of the key features of the 'concept of the vocation' (*Berufskonzept*) comprises the major elements for what is regarded – in the German context – as the necessary framework of a training system that primarily aims to develop and deepen the capability of the individual to work and act competently in a vocational environment (*berufliche Handlungsfähigkeit*) (Table II).

Qualified work
Professional, methodical and social competences for planning, executing and controlling vocational tasks.

Broad vocational basis
Multilayered, marketable pattern of competences relevant not only for the training company through a broad knowledge basis and skills specifically related to the occupation.

Adaptable skills
Skills are responsive to a changing vocational environment and represent an appropriate basis for further training and lifelong learning.

Mobility
National, state-recognised occupations decrease workers' dependence on one employer; labour mobility is enhanced.

Transparency
Recognised occupations and their value in the educational system are accepted and well known by employers and employees.

Social security
Qualification in a recognised occupation ensures a high degree of social security and determines to a certain extent social status.

Table II. Key features of the 'concept of the vocation' in Germany.[31]

During the early 1990s, experts in the field began to question whether the 'concept of the vocation' was still the right basis for the German training system. Whereas the merits of the concept for reconstruction and development after economic crises and wars are unanimously acknowledged, some observers doubt its potential to respond to the modernisation pressures of a rapidly changing economic environment (Geissler, 1994, p. 328). The most important consequence of this process of change for VET is the decreasing value of initial qualifications, whereas further training and lifelong learning are more and more crucial in any worker's career. In their article 'At the End of the Vocation', Geissler & Orthey (1998) argue that vocations will be replaced by quickly adaptable 'packages of skills' that are based on 'meta-competences', with the ability and willingness to learn constantly being the most important of these.

Will these developments inevitably lead to the end of vocations as such? Undoubtedly, the initial qualification of a young person is the starting point for further periods of learning and training rather than the end of education and training, as was the case in former times.[32] The shortened half-life times of skills and knowledge mean that career prospects and social status are no longer determined by a person's initial qualification; this is even true for a vocationally structured society like that of Germany. The vocation as the destined path of each human being, defined by vocational educationists as the ultimate goal in life and the first aim of education in the 1920s (cf. Spranger, 1920), is quite outdated.

However, as a necessary and decisive basis for a lifelong learning process, solid knowledge and skills seem to be more important than ever before. The ability to react to a rapidly changing work environment can only be acquired in comprehensive learning processes (as shown in appendix I) which prepare young people for a variety of future tasks. In order to achieve this, vocations must not be interpreted as static concepts but must be continuously adapted to the needs of changing economies and societies. Therefore, making best use of its inherent potentials for flexibility, instead of misusing it as a blocking instrument to prevent any attempts to modernise training provision, seems to be the right approach towards the 'concept of the vocation' today. In the absence of a structural and functional alternative to this concept (Kutscha, 1992, p. 538), its modernisation is also the only promising way forward to remedy the current symptoms of crisis in the VET system.

The Challenge of Modernisation

The Dual System of VET in Germany is called into question by many educationists for a variety of reasons. The future prospects of the system are the subject of great controversy.[33] Arguments in favour of a sceptical position are provided by the symptoms of crisis in the training sector: decreasing appeal of the Dual System to potential trainees, declining willingness of employers to provide training places [34], drastically dwindling state resources for training (Münk, 1997, p. 8). The challenges the Dual System is facing seem to be enormous: rising educational standards, increasing heterogeneity of trainees, higher demands on training, higher average age of trainees, changing training conditions in companies (Keune & Zielke, 1992, p. 32; Georg, 1997, p. 314). Undoubtedly, these challenges do not only concern the Dual System but are rooted in changing social conditions affecting the main structures of the whole educational system.[35] The changing relationship between general and vocational education may represent the most prominent example for this transitional phase in education.

In vocational education, however, the solution to these problems is to create more flexible structures for training. Flexibility in this context means primarily responsiveness to the *changing work environment* and responsiveness to the *varying personal potentials* of trainees in the form of individualised training pathways (Sloane, 1997a, p. 231). Most frequently, educationists suggest measures of deregulation and differentiation to create flexibility in the two forms mentioned.[36] More decision-making processes at a regional or local level and differentiated training paths, both integrated in a national framework, would be needed. Modularisation as a regulatory framework is regarded as one way in which both aims could be achieved.

To summarise, it can be argued that the structure of the training sector, based on the 'concept of the vocation', has proved to be successful in Germany over a period of some hundred years. Although time and again people have predicted the imminent end of the system and its underlying principles, it has turned out that the new challenges were met by changes within the system rather than by developing an entirely new system. Bearing this in mind, it seems reasonably safe to argue that current challenges in the German training sector will be met by a cautious process of modernisation within the system rather than by replacing it. Modularisation in VET is frequently mentioned as one of the reforming steps. The assessment of the potential of modules to reform the training system and to form a new regulative framework in Germany is the overall subject of this study. A conceptualisation of modularisation seems to represent the first step towards reaching a valid conclusion to this question. How much potential do different forms of modularisation have for the VET system of Germany?

CHAPTER 3

The Concept of Modularisation

A Definition of Modules in Education

Defining the nature of modules in education is no easy task. Some of the definitions given in appendix II [37] suggest that there is no generally accepted explanation of what is meant by organising the teaching/learning process in modules (Postlethwait, 1985; Schmidt, 1997a; Kloas, 1997b). Nevertheless, it seems to be generally accepted that any definition can only be valid and appropriate in the normative context in which it has been developed. A description of the way a module in VET is to be constructed and embedded in a wider curricular framework, its intended function and its didactical structure are inextricably linked with the approach one takes towards VET.

Following the technical origins of the term, there seems to be agreement that a module is a part of a bigger entity or system. In this context, a modularised system is a discrete whole composed of a number of self-contained elements. Concerning modularisation in VET, the definitions in appendix II vary decisively in the degree to which they refer to the relationship between the system as a whole and modules as elements of the whole. Some definitions emphasise the self-contained character of modules: they cover 'a single conceptual unit of subject matter' (Postlethwait, 1985), they 'are complete in themselves and examinable as such' (Wiegand, 1996b) and independent from other curricular elements (Deissinger, 1996a).

The other group of definitions stresses that educational modules can fulfil their envisaged purpose only in the context of other parts of the system: they are primarily 'part of a whole' (Schmidt, 1997a). The 'whole' in the context of VET may be a qualification in the broadest sense, which itself is embedded in 'the horizontal and vertical structure of a qualification system' (Reuling & Sauter, 1996). For the attainment of a qualification, 'a designated number of modules is required' (Theodossin, 1986). In this line of argument, 'modules only have a logic in terms of the broader qualifications and set of awards of which they form a part' (Nasta, 1994). In terms of the curriculum design process, the latter definitions of modules entail a process which starts with considering the qualification as a whole before considering its elements. The learner's choice is essentially between one course of study or another. If the former approach towards modules is taken, the building of a curriculum starts from the design of the individual modules and the learner chooses a certain combination of modules instead of a discrete qualification.[38]

The contradiction of modules as basically free-standing and modules as only valuable in the context of the wider structure of a qualification may be overcome by the 'built-up effect', as suggested by Ainley (1990): 'a module can stand alone *or* form a part of a route picked through the various units on offer', or by Schmidt (1997b): 'Combining them [modules] like building blocks, they *can* form an overall qualification' (author's emphasis).[39] This notion seems to be in line with the 'twofold character' attributed to educational modules by Sloane, who regards modules as wholes in themselves but also requires them 'to be embedded into a "bigger whole"'.

In order to clarify the relationship between modules and qualifications in VET and to generate further characteristics of a modularised training arrangement, the approach of Kloas (1997b, pp. 12–16) is adopted. In his very vivid illustration, Kloas explains the nature of modules in education by comparing them with the components that form a building. In his example, the building represents the system. Importantly, this system's aim – and, therefore, the superordinate aim of modularisation – is the notion of the ability of the individual to act and work competently in the occupational environment of the world of work (*berufliche Handlungsfähigkeit*). This notion of the individual's 'vocational competence', however, is closely linked to the 'concept of the vocation' which determines VET in Germany and which was explained in chapter 2. As a result of his explanation from a German point of view, Kloas defines modules in VET by the characteristics summarised in Table III.

The terminology is confusing, both in the British, and in the German, context. Moreover, it is unclear in many cases if the words 'unit' and 'module' are used interchangeably or to mark a difference. The most widely accepted English definition of these terms explains a *unit* as 'a coherent set of learning outcomes' and a *module* as 'a sub set of a learning programme' (Further Education Unit [FEU], 1995). In the German discussion, both of these meanings are normally ascribed to the term *Modul*; in most cases, a word for the aforementioned meaning of 'unit' is not even needed as German vocational qualifications are not defined in outcomes (see chapter 2). Nevertheless, a German term for 'unit' could be necessary in the future, if modularity gains more influence on educational provision.

Integrative function
The overall qualification consists of a combination of modules or part-qualifications respectively. This combination of modules generates the qualification's function (which is the 'vocational competence' of the individual). This overall function is more than the sum of the single functions of the part-qualifications. Some modules may be utilisable independently from the overall function. This characteristic cannot, however, substitute the overall function of a qualification.

Standard definition
The capability to work competently in an occupational environment is defined by social and economic standards. Some modules are indispensable for basic standards in VET, others improve the individual's capability to work in a highly sophisticated environment.[40]

Outcome orientation
Modules are the result of a qualification process and are only of value if they contribute to the overall function of the qualification. Therefore, modules represent categories of outcome or competence.

Restricted variability
The variability of the temporal sequence of modules is restricted by pedagogic criteria and inherent content structures.

Accepted standards
Modules are not thinkable without standards ensuring comparability and intelligibility. These standards are the precondition for the combination of modules leading to recognised qualifications.

General standards
The standard of modules needs to be relevant for more than only one or a few companies and providers of qualifications.

Multiple relevance
Modular systems in VET are effective if modules are relevant to several areas of occupation.

Additional competences
Modules required for a certain vocation can be augmented by additional modules in order to improve the vocational perspectives of the learner. Accepted standards of modules are the precondition for supplementing the overall function of a qualification.

Individual modification
Single modules can be modified, replaced and adapted without changing the overall qualification.

Table III. Characteristics of modules in VET.[41]

Concepts of Modularisation in the German Context

As highlighted in the introduction, the debate about modules in German VET is controversial and far from being settled. In the debate, it often remains unclear what concept of modularisation is under scrutiny. Therefore, an attempt should be made to identify conceivable types of modular structures for the German system of initial training.[42]

In the first concept, the existing provisions for initial training in the Dual System or in school-based training are supplemented by additional competences. In this *expansion concept*, modules assume the function of coherent and self-contained part-qualifications on top of the 'normal' qualification. The overall function of the qualification is expanded. In practice, the initial training is augmented by extra skills, which are normally the subject of further education and training.[43] In many cases, these provisions are used to make vocational training more attractive to young people with university entrance qualifications. In general, this target group has the opportunity to take advantage of shortened apprenticeship periods. If they decide to stay in training in a pilot scheme of the type described for the full period of training (in most cases between 3 and 3½ years), they have the chance to acquire extra qualifications (cf., for example, Braukmann & Sloane, 1994, p. 37ff.) In terms of the organisation of these pilot schemes, there are two basic variants.

In the *consecutive model,* the contents of initial and further training remain separated. The modules leading to the extra qualifications are isolated from the teaching/learning sequences referring to the basic qualification. In extreme cases, the isolation is emphasised by the institutional separation, i.e. different institutions are responsible for the components of initial training (vocational schools, training companies) and further training (providers of further education and training like Chambers of Industry and Commerce, Crafts Chambers).[44] The consequence of the institutional separation is a lack of coherence on the micro-didactic level. The trainees are confronted with different and often incompatible teaching styles, learning objectives and pedagogic methodologies of the different providers.

The *integrative model* tries to overcome the disadvantageous effects of this separation. The contents of initial and further training are integrated in an overall concept; the result is a newly structured qualification. A precondition for the integration of the contents is the close cooperation of the institutions involved in the training. Experiences in pilot schemes show, however, that teachers and trainers tend to stick to their roles in the old structures, in which initial and further training are strictly separated. Therefore, they fail to translate the integration of contents, which is planned at the macro-didactic level, into their day-to-day work at the micro-didactic level. In such cases, the envisaged integrative model is likely to revert back to the easier-to-handle consecutive model.[45]

In both models, the regulative framework of initial training (*Ausbildungsordnung, Rahmenlehrplan*) remains unaffected if the adaptation of the additional parts of the qualifications seems necessary as a consequence of technical and economic changes. Furthermore, the broad design of recognised German qualifications can be focused by the additional modules. Particular requirements of companies in a certain area and the individual educational needs of trainees can be taken into account when additional modules are designed. The expansion concept makes use of several functions/characteristics of modules in VET as derived in the previous section ('multiple relevance', 'additional competences', 'individual modification') to develop more flexible and individualised provisions within the strictly regulated German system of initial training. Not surprisingly, this concept seems to have strong support from German industry.[46]

In a second concept of modularisation, the existing qualifications of initial training are reorganised into a modular system. The modularisation in this *differentiation concept* would restructure the curricula of the qualifications with the result that self-contained elements would only be marketable if they were combined with all other necessary components leading to an overall qualification (cf. Haack et al, 1996, p. 9ff.) Modules arise from the dismantling of complex vocational profiles into smaller, differentiated parts, which can be assessed and credited individually.[47] Characteristically, an overall qualification requires a defined set of modules. As they are only marketable as part of such a set, the freedom to combine modules is restricted. In this concept, the same modules are used for different qualifications within one occupational area. Therefore, the acquisition of more than one qualification becomes easier as such shared modules would be accredited if a trainee starts to work towards a second qualification which is related to a previous one. If a trainee is not able to finish the overall qualification, it is possible to record the credited modules for a later continuation of the training or as part of a different qualification.[48] In the English context, this procedure is covered by the phrase 'accreditation of prior learning' (APL).

In Germany, the differentiation concept can also be seen in the context of the debate about the linking of general and vocational education. The idea of the equality of general and vocational education was the basis for the *Kollegschule* [49], a kind of pilot school set up in North Rhine-Westphalia, in which the university entrance qualification (*Abitur*) and a vocational qualification (*Facharbeiterbrief*) could be obtained at the same time (Blankertz, 1972a; Schenk, 1992; Jank & Meyer, 1994, p. 374ff.) The potential of modular structures to facilitate the acquisition of post-compulsory qualifications across the academic/vocational divide can be identified in the use of the same basic modules for vocational and academic pathways.[50]

This sharing of modules for academic and vocational qualifications as well as for several occupational qualifications demands that modules are outcome-oriented and contribute to the overall function of the qualification aspired to, and that their standards are defined by social and economic measures (cf. the assumptions under the subheadings 'integrative function', 'standard definition' and 'outcome orientation' in Table III). The obvious advantages of the differentiation concept are its use of existing qualifications (which only need to be transferred into a modular structure), its opportunities for flexible and individualised routes to qualifications which may bridge the gulf between vocational and academic careers, and its increased efficiency as a result of the multiple relevance of modules.

A precondition to fully develop the potential advantages of the differentiation concept is an instrument for recording successfully completed modules, which does not yet exist in Germany. The idea of such a *Berufsbildungspaß* is criticised, as it would establish a level of qualifications below the existing system of recognised qualifications. Furthermore, the experiences with the *Kollegschule* show that there is a danger that teaching styles and methods of schools leading to an academic career are simply transferred to provisions in vocational education as soon as vocational qualifications confer the right to study at university.[51]

Contrary to the expansion and differentiation concept, the third concept is not conceivable in the existing regulatory framework of German VET. In this *fragmentation concept*, modules are not only self-contained and can be assessed and credited individually, but are also marketable outside an overall qualification. Modules can be combined freely, without the restriction of fitting into a defined qualification. Generally, it is the trainee who defines her or his qualification. In the German context, this concept is incompatible with the 'concept of the vocation' and overcomes traditional structures of educational stages, achievement measurement and assessment. The overall function of the existing qualifications would no longer be valid; the qualifications would be fragmented.

As modules are independently marketable and combinable, the trainee can react quickly to the changing requirements of the occupational environment. Therefore, this concept makes full use of the opportunities of a modularised system resulting from the advantage of individual modification and addition of modules. This represents a potential of modular structures that cannot be overestimated in times of the increasingly devalued marketability of initial training due to shorter technical innovation cycles and widespread organisation restructuring schemes in companies.[52] Individual learning deficits of trainees can be taken into account more specifically, e.g. by creating repetition modules for the most common learning difficulties of certain target groups.

The fragmentation concept integrates initial and further training and opens new possibilities for a lifelong and work-accompanying learning system, as the traditional lines of demarcation between the different areas of learning are obsolete. For training companies, this means that training can take the particular circumstances of the company into account to a greater extent than within the existing structures. Providers who are able to anticipate qualification needs and offer up-to-date modules would benefit from this highly flexible concept. The main dangers are the fragmentation and the lack of cohesion of the whole system, which could lead to difficulties in the marketability of qualifications (Haack et al, 1996, p. 10; Reuling, 1996, p. 49).

Undoubtedly, the fragmentation concept is not compatible with several of the characteristics of modularisation in VET as developed in the previous section. Most importantly, it contradicts the integrative function ascribed to modules. This contradiction is inevitable as the overall function of qualifications, the 'vocational competence' of the individual, is derived from the German 'concept of the vocation', which is incompatible with the fragmentation concept. For the same reason, the concept contradicts the relevance of social norms for the definition of accepted and general standards for modules. Compared to the two concepts explained earlier, it is primarily the fragmentation concept which is the cause of controversial debate in Germany (cf. Zentralverband des Deutschen Handwerks [ZDH], 1993, p. 128; Zedler, 1996, p. 20ff. and 1997, p. 42; Schmidt, 1997b, p. 42).

Although there are restrictions in the way units are combined to achieve certain levels of NVQs and GNVQs, and despite the fact that there are procedures to set standards for these units 'for breadth of application' (National Council for Vocational Qualifications [NCVQ], 1995, p. 16), German observers categorise the English system of VET as representing a fragmentation concept (Deissinger, 1996a, pp. 194–198; Sloane, 1997a, p. 230; Kloas, 1997b, p. 11). It will be discussed later whether this categorisation is justifiable or not, but obviously the English system does contradict the German 'concept of the vocation' and, therefore, some of the characteristics/functions of modules derived from this principle in the previous section. For a sensible discussion of modularisation and of the fragmentation concept in particular, it seems necessary to identify the key ideas that determine VET in Germany and England. Only with these ideas in mind is it possible to assess the potential for a modularised system in Germany. As we have seen, the fragmentation concept is of particular interest because it offers the most opportunities for a flexible and individualised system of VET in the post-Fordist area. As the English provisions represent a version of this concept in practice, NVQs and GNVQs seem to be the best alternative example for a discussion about the reform of German provisions. The expansion and the differentiation concepts are significant as they offer some potential for a more flexible and individualised system within the existing regulatory framework and, further, because they have already been tested to a certain extent in the German context.

Before concentrating on the provisions in England, it seems necessary to shed light on the debate about modularisation from a European perspective; and – as a conclusion to this section – Table IV gives an overview of the three concepts of modularisation developed here and which are to be used in the following argumentation.

Expansion concept
Modules supplement initial training qualifications to generate additional competences that are typically the subject of further education and training. The overall functions of initial qualifications are expanded.

There are two types of organisational implementation: In the consecutive model, the contents of initial and further training remain separated. In the integrative model, the contents of further training are integrated into the initial qualification.

Differentiation concept
Modules are the result of restructuring the curricula of existing qualifications. The framework of the overall qualification regulates the combination of modules. Modules are self-contained and can be assessed and credited individually, but they are only marketable as part of an overall qualification.

Like the expansion concept, the differentiation concept does not contradict the existing regulatory framework of German initial training.

Fragmentation concept
Modules are marketable without the framework of an overall qualification. By combining modules freely, trainees create individualised qualifications that mirror the requirements of a rapidly changing occupational environment.

In comparison to the expansion and the differentiation concept, the fragmentation concept offers the greatest opportunities for a maximum of flexibility and individuality in VET. Unlike the other two concepts, it is not consistent with the German 'concept of the vocation'.

Table IV. Concepts of modularisation in VET.

CHAPTER 4

Modularisation of Vocational Education in a European Perspective

The Provisions of the European Union in the Field of Vocational Education and Training

The competence of the EU in the field of vocational education and training has developed in a sequence of steps.[53] In contrast to general education, training was explicitly mentioned in the Treaties of Rome (1957) [54], which ordered the European Council to:

> *lay down general principles for implementing a common vocational training policy capable of contributing to the harmonious development both of the national economies and of the common market (Treaty on EEC, Art. 128);*

and

> *the Commission shall have the task of promoting close co-operation between Member States in ... basic and advanced vocational training. (Art. 118)*

It was not until 1963 that the Council began to meet the requirements of Article 128, when it agreed on 10 general principles for setting up a common policy for vocational education and training (Decision 63/226 of 2 April 1963). However, owing to arguments about the legal character of the principles (Flynn, 1988; Barnard, 1995, p. 14ff.), cooperation between European countries in the field took place at an intergovernmental rather than at a supranational level.

Consequently, joint action in vocational education was very limited in the 1960s. The situation changed somewhat after the Janne Report of 1973 stipulated for the first time a new relationship between general and vocational education:

> *there is no longer any good vocational training that does not comprise a sound general training at all levels, and there is no longer any good general training which is not linked with concrete practice, and, in principle, with real work. (Janne Report, quoted in Neave, 1984, p. 62)*

For general education, the findings of the Janne Report stimulated the Education Action Programme passed by the Council of Ministers in 1976, which can be seen as the foundation of cooperation in general education (Commission of the European Communities, 1993, p. 17; Brock & Tulasiewicz, 1994, p. 7; Delgado & Losa, 1997, p. 131ff.) The establishment of the European Centre for the Development of Vocational Education (CEDEFOP) in West Berlin in 1975 (moved to Thessaloniki, Greece, in 1995) was an indirect consequence of the Report in the field of vocational education, and proved central to new initiatives. In particular, CEDEFOP prepared the ground for the definition of five EU-wide levels of vocational qualifications and certificates (EC Decision 85/386 of June 1985). These levels constitute the framework for mutual recognition and transparency of qualifications in the member states (Zimmermann, 1993, p. 338; Wiegand, 1996a, p. 262ff.) Most prominently, CEDEFOP initiated on the basis of the level framework a comparability exercise which resulted in the SEDOC register of more than 200 comparable occupational activities.[55]

However, it was the ruling of the European Court of Justice, which interpreted Article 128 of the Treaty on the EEC in favour of extended competences of Community bodies, that encouraged the Community to initiate more activities in the field of vocational education and training from the mid-1980s onwards.[56] As a result of this policy, the Community launched a series of programmes in education.[57] In the field of vocational training, the two most important programmes were those which stimulated opportunities for training after compulsory schooling (European Community Action Programme for the Vocational Training of Young People and Their Preparation for Adult and Working Life – PETRA) and encouraged cooperation between universities and industry for training in technology (European Community Action Programme in Education and Training for Technology – COMETT). Reorganised and restructured as a preparation for the Single European Act (SEA), which established the Single European Market in 1993, such projects and programmes have enhanced Europeanised learning opportunities for individuals and institutions within the Community.

As the legal basis for these initiatives seemed to be unclear, the Treaty on European Union (Maastricht Treaty) dealt with vocational training (Art. 127) and for the first time in an explicit way, with general education (Art. 126).[58] Both Articles are similarly structured and explicitly exclude 'any harmonization of the laws and regulations of the Member States' (Art. 126[4], Art. 127[4]). These clauses mirror the principle of subsidiarity, stated in Article 3b (cf. Rudden & Wyatt, 1994, p. 29). According to the principle of subsidiarity:

> *the Community shall take action ... only if and in so far as the objectives of the proposed action cannot be sufficiently achieved by the Member States and can therefore, ... be better achieved by the Community. (Art. 3b)*

In vocational training, therefore, the Community is only entitled to:

> *implement a vocational training policy which shall support and supplement the action of the Member States. (Art. 127[1])*

The subsequent paragraphs in Article 127 specify the role of the Community to facilitate cooperation between member states (para. 2) and with third countries and competent international organisations (para. 3).

The Treaty of Maastricht and its consequences for vocational education and training have been discussed and interpreted widely by experts in the field as well as being debated in Community institutions in recent years.[59] On the one hand, it is argued that Article 127 merely underpins the status quo of competences increasingly assumed by the Commission and Council over the last two decades (Delgado & Losa, 1997, pp. 142ff., 167; Hörner, 1997, p. 67) and that an opportunity was missed to create a European framework for VET (Geissler, 1994, p. 323ff.) A different line of argumentation, however, emphasises the combined effects of the Treaty's provisions, which make exchange of information and mobility of labour possible on a wider scale and promote the compatibility of national systems (ETUCE, 1995, p. 18ff.) On the basis of the Treaty, the LEONARDO DA VINCI programme was launched in 1994, covering and extending the activities in the field of vocational training, formerly supported by the programmes PETRA, FORCE (Formation Continue en Europe), EUROTECNET (European Technology Network for Training), LINGUA (Programme for the Promotion of Foreign Language Knowledge in the European Community), IRIS (European Community Network of Training Programmes for Women) and COMETT.[60] After an initial period of time devoted to developing bilateral exchange programmes and information networks, the LEONARDO programme then shifted its emphasis to multilateral actions considered beneficial for the training sector in the whole Union and with the aim of integrating initial and further education (Fahle, 1995, p. 26ff.; Bender, 1995, pp. 21–24). LEONARDO was extended recently for the 7-year period between 2000 and 2006. LEONARDO II continues the successful actions of the first generation in a substantially streamlined organisational structure and with increased funding.

The effects of the current development of multilingual training profiles and the EUROPASS training, both aimed at the increase of workers' mobility have to be awaited (Benner, 1997b; Herz & Jäger, 1998, p. 15).

However, Europe-wide or comparable vocational qualifications are not likely to be on the EU agenda in the near future. Yet, modular structures in vocational education and training might facilitate the creation of a more cohesive system of contents and qualifications in the field (Rützel, 1997, p. 9).

Beyond the Maastricht Treaty: convergence pressures in VET

The question of whether Article 127 of the Maastricht Treaty has to be regarded as the 'last word' of the EU in the field of VET has been a matter of extensive discussion over the last few years. The issue of whether or not the Union should assume more competences in the field is highly controversial. However these questions are answered, the need for increased compatibility of vocational qualifications and more transparent vocational systems is widely acknowledged. Two main reasons for this necessity can be identified.

Consequences of the economic convergence. It has been argued many times that social policy in general and educational policy in particular has been regarded as a means of attaining the economic aims of the European Community right from the very start of the Community (cf., for example, Rubio, 1997, p. 72ff.) – a fact which was not changed by the Maastricht Treaty (Feuchthofen, 1993, p. 74ff.; Münk, 1995, pp. 31–34). The envisaged unrestricted mobility of goods, services and capital within the European Monetary Union requires a mobile workforce.[61] Consequently, the qualification systems in the member states will be more in competition with each other than ever before. Moreover, standardisation and harmonisation will be required of vocational qualifications, in a manner similar to that which was imposed on production methods within export markets a long time ago. The creation of equivalent qualifications, the EU-wide recognition of national qualifications and the introduction of European qualification levels which facilitate the classification of foreign vocational certificates mirror this need for comparability.[62] As a spin-off of EU initiatives to create a regulatory framework for mutual recognition of qualifications (pushed ahead by CEDEFOP), reforms of national regulations tend to be oriented towards the European classification of qualifications (Cleve & Kell, 1996, p. 16). The influence of EU policies in VET on national provisions is undeniable. Comparable challenges to national economies because of the ever more closely linked global markets increase the likelihood that similar strategies are applied to modernise training provisions (Georg, 1997, p. 313).

Political will of EU bodies to converge national systems. Despite the clear exclusion of any harmonisation of national educational provisions in the Maastricht Treaty (Art. 127[4], 126[4]), the Council of the EU demanded that general and vocational education systems within the Union undergo a process of far-reaching convergence.[63] This demand seems to be incompatible with the principle of subsidiarity (Art. 3b); nevertheless, a move towards a more 'dynamic' interpretation of subsidiarity by the European Commission can be seen to have emerged even before the Maastricht Treaty was passed. In the *Memorandum of Vocational Training in the EC in the 1990s*, the dynamic attitude towards subsidiarity was described by the aim of combining national and supranational policies (Commission of the European Communities, 1991, p. 13, para. 48). Based on Article 5 (Maastricht Treaty), which requires the member states to orient national measures towards the objectives of the Union, this line of argumentation justifies involvement of the EU institutions to a much wider extent (Koch, 1994, p. 28). Consequently, resolutions, decisions and directives of EU bodies, most importantly of the Commission, could assert convergence pressure on national systems of vocational education. The proposals for new methods of transnational validation of competences in the 1996 *White Paper on Education and Training: teaching and learning* may be seen as an outcome of this policy (European Commission, 1996, pp. 53–56; Beckers, 1997, p. 217ff.) Despite these pressures for comparable systems of vocational education in the EU, the member states seem to be extremely reluctant to give up their autonomy to regulate training provisions.[64] In this ambivalent situation – pressures for a more harmonised system on the one hand and insistence on national autonomy on the other – the trend towards modular structures in training may lead the way out of this dilemma and make it possible to embark on joint strategies in VET. As described in chapter 3, modularisation can contribute to the integration of formerly separated sectors in education, e.g. initial and further training and general and vocational education. This 'integrative potential' [65] of modular systems may also bridge the divide between national qualification systems (Rützel, 1997, p. 9). One possibility could be the joint development of modules that are used in more than one country. Before assessing this possibility, it will be necessary to investigate the existing approaches towards modularisation in some of the EU member states.

Approaches towards Modularisation in EU Member States

At the beginning of the 1990s, a 2-year project conducted by experts from six EU member countries (France, Germany, Luxembourg, the Netherlands, Scotland and Spain) investigated the use of modules in initial vocational training. The main aim of this project, promoted by the

EU programme PETRA, was to identify different forms of modularisation in the aforementioned countries. By interviewing teachers from vocational schools and trainers from training companies, different approaches to putting modular concepts into practice were identified. Table V describes modular concepts in VET in four countries that were part of the project. This selection is based on the fact that modularisation seems to be more advanced in these countries than in most other EU member states. Furthermore, the findings derived from interviews with practitioners seem to give a more reliable picture than mere descriptive accounts of official policies.[66]

	Spain	France	Netherlands [67]	Scotland
Scope of modularisation	Entire system of VET	Only for certain target groups	Certain economic sectors (e.g. qualifications in printing industry)	Entire system of VET
Target group(s)	Ranging from school-leavers to adult workers	Disadvantaged or unemployed juveniles (CFI)	All workers in the printing industry	Ranging from school-leavers to adult workers
Main aims of modularisation	Equality and integration of general and vocational education Revitalisation of the initial training sector	(Re)integration of specific target groups in regular training provisions Competence in self-conducted learning (learning to learn)	Increase of flexibility and responsiveness of training provisions Integration of initial and continuing training	Creation of a single cohesive qualification framework Increase of flexibility of training provisions
Duration of modules	Up to 1200 hours	40 hours	Variable	40 hours
Marketability of modules	Marketable as part-qualifications	Not marketable individually	Marketable only as part of an overall vocational qualification	In principle marketable individually but advantage of group awards
Combination of modules	Unrestricted combination to wider qualifications possible	Combination of modules into clusters	The combination of 8 modules chosen from 4 fields constitute an overall qualification	Modules combined to group awards (SVQs, GSVQs)
Other characteristics of modules	Self-contained Modules classified for different levels Sharing of modules possible Flexible order of accreditation	Clusters describe three levels: 1. remedial measures 2. vocational preparation 3. vocational qualification	Free choice from modules offered in different fields Upgrading of overall qualification by additional modules possible Flexible order of accreditation	3 types of modules: NC-modules, SVQs, GSVQs Contents of modules defined in learning outcomes Self-sufficient units Flexible order of accreditation Sharing of modules possible
Responsibility	Responsibility of provincial administration in cooperation with employers and trade unions	Centralised state regulation of all important programmes in VET [68]	Sector-specific national bodies (GOC for the graphic industry), ruled by social partners and educationists	SCOTVEC awards all individual modules and group awards, decisive influence of industry on SVQs
Concept of modularisation [69]	Fragmentation concept	Fragmentation concept (for the sector of vocational preparation of specific target groups)	Differentiation concept (in initial training), Expansion concept (in continuing training)	Fragmentation concept

Table V. Approaches towards modularisation of VET in four European countries.

The four modular strategies are described in more detail in appendix IV. In line with the approach taken throughout this study, this section and appendix IV gives a brief account of different approaches towards modularisation in VET and the understanding that different strategies are successful in different economic and educational conditions. As a result of these conditions, modularisation fulfils different functions, is employed to achieve different aims and faces different problems. Read in the context of chapter 3, the juxtaposition provides and illustrates examples for the characteristics of modules and concepts of modularisation that were developed earlier. For the reform of initial training in Germany, the practice in other countries may provide starting-points for the development of an approach towards modularisation which takes the specific circumstances of the German legal framework into account.

Moreover, the examples from other countries may overcome the often-expressed fear of an incoherent, confusing and fragmented system of VET as the inevitable consequence of modular reforms. Yet, one of the main findings of the EU project was that in almost all cases modules were designed to integrate competences and knowledge in order to enable the trainee to meet the challenges of the vocational environment. Even in countries which follow the fragmentation concept of modularisation (cf. chapter 3), such as Spain and Scotland, the investigators reached this somewhat surprising conclusion (Manning, 1994, p. 40).

Finally, it is not possible, without taking the national approaches into account, to regard modularisation as a strategy to bring VET systems in the EU closer together, to make transition between them easier and to make mutual recognition of qualifications transparent. This is also necessary for the joint development of European modules in VET, the subject of the next section.

'European Modules' as a Way of Enhancing the European Dimension in VET

In the discussions concerning the integration process in Europe, the implementation of a European dimension in education is frequently proposed as a way forward. Although the term first appeared in the 1976 EC Action Programme of Education (see the first section of this chapter; Ryba, 1992, p. 11), the concept of a European dimension was not further specified until 1988, when the Council of Ministers agreed on a formal definition.[70]

The general aims of this concept are to enhance young people's awareness of their European identity and to prepare them to take part in the economic and social development of the Community, to create awareness of the advantages of and challenges to the Community, to improve knowledge of the Community as well as of the individual member states, and to emphasise the importance of cooperation with the wider international community.

The Maastricht Treaty takes up the concept for general education in Article 126(2), stating the aim of 'developing the European dimension in education, particularly through the teaching and dissemination of the languages of the Member States'. The Treaty does not, however, specify the precise meaning of the concept, nor does it suggest ways in which it could be put into practice (Lagner, 1997, p. 26ff.) This lack of operationalised objectives is at the root of the failure to influence educational practices in the member states by introducing a European dimension to national provision.[71] The 1993 European Commission's *Green Paper on the European Dimension of Education* elaborates primarily on aspects of contributing to European citizenship, improving the quality of education and integrating young people into society and working life (Commission of the European Communities, 1993, p. 6ff.) However, yet again, the suggestions given for achieving these goals (for instance, learning languages, transnational projects, socialisation of youngsters in a European context, cooperation of schools, partnership networks) remain rather vague. Most importantly, the principle of subsidiarity rules out a more concrete conceptualisation of the European dimension and leaves it to the highly diverse implementation approaches of the member states (Ryba, 1992, p. 18ff.; Lagner, 1997, p. 30).

In VET, efforts to improve the quality of training and the promotion of mobility and comparability of qualifications in the Single European Market (SEM) seem to be central to the concept of a European dimension (Commission of the European Communities, 1990, p. 51). Despite the overarching aim of the LEONARDO programme to develop the European dimension in vocational education, the implementation of the concept in national training provisions appears to be unsystematic and often fragmented. 'European Modules', i.e. part-qualifications which prepare young people for employment in the common market and which can be incorporated into the national training provisions, may lead the way to a more coherent framework for the efficient implementation of the European dimension.

Commentators regard such modules as beneficial and acceptable from the perspective of the member states, as they could be developed in EU programmes like LEONARDO and would supplement national provisions (Wiegand, 1996a, p. 271; 1995, p. 29). Sellin (1994b, p. 8) mentions in this context, the development of modules within projects like PETRA II, FORCE and EUROFORM (European Community Framework for New Skills and New Employment Opportunities Induced by Technological Change and the Single Market).[72]

The additional qualification for apprentices of the Hüls AG represents an example of such European modules in Germany. From 1992 onwards, the company started to cooperate with partners from Finland, Ireland, Norway, Sweden and the United Kingdom in the development of modules which supplement the regular initial training of their apprentices. The modules cover general knowledge about living and working in Europe, and languages, as well as skills specifically related to the trainees' occupations (Cleve, 1995, p. 14).

Although not explicitly organised in modules, the pilot project EUWAS (*Euro-WirtschaftsassistentIn*) may be regarded as belonging to the same category (Lagner, 1997). It provides an additional qualification for trainees in the business and commerce sector in North Rhine–Westphalia and is organised into six self-sustained learning areas. Therefore, similarities to the expansion concept of modularisation are striking. One aim of this pilot project is explicitly to integrate the European dimension into training. The additional content is related to the specific occupational field of the trainees to a closer extent than in the first example.

Providing additional content to initial training qualifications, these two approaches represent examples of the expansion concept of modularisation as explained in chapter 3. Modules of this kind are not binding for member states but offer additional part-qualifications on top of regular qualifications provided by national training systems. Sellin (1994b, p. 8) regrets that projects of this kind have not yet been incorporated into the standard training systems of the countries taking part. Any move by EU institutions to make European modules obligatory would obviously be contradictory to Article 127(1) of the Maastricht Treaty:

> *The Community shall ... supplement the action of the Member States, while fully respecting the responsibility of the Member States for the content and organization of vocational training.*

Contrary to Sellin, Sloane (1993, p. 105) argues that a binding character of European modules is not desirable as the structure of modules must be flexible enough to be responsive to the needs of individual training companies at a specific point in time. The merits of a high degree of openness of European provisions in general and in relation to the European dimension in particular, is a weighty argument for a modularised structure of European contents, as modules are more easily adaptable than traditional overall course structures. Based on an empirical survey in Germany, in which senior staff of craft institutions (e.g. Chamber of Crafts) and 100 master craftsmen were questioned, Sloane identifies the need for two different levels of cooperation, which would develop, implement, revise and adapt European modules in member states. The *first level* represents the cooperation between education and training organisations of the countries involved. At this level, the adaptation of modules to national needs and the creation of acceptance of the modules take place. A *second level of cooperation*, involving representatives from training companies and trade unions, would assume responsibility for the adaptation of the modules for the needs of individual training companies and specific occupations.[73] A further finding of the survey is that the overwhelming majority of practitioners argue that European modules should supplement the existing provisions for initial training in craft trades rather than replace them.

Interpreting the findings of his empirical research, Sloane goes on to develop a didactic structure of European modules which would not only allow the systematic creation of modules but also their adaptation on the two levels of cooperation described. His model may be described as shown in Figure 2.

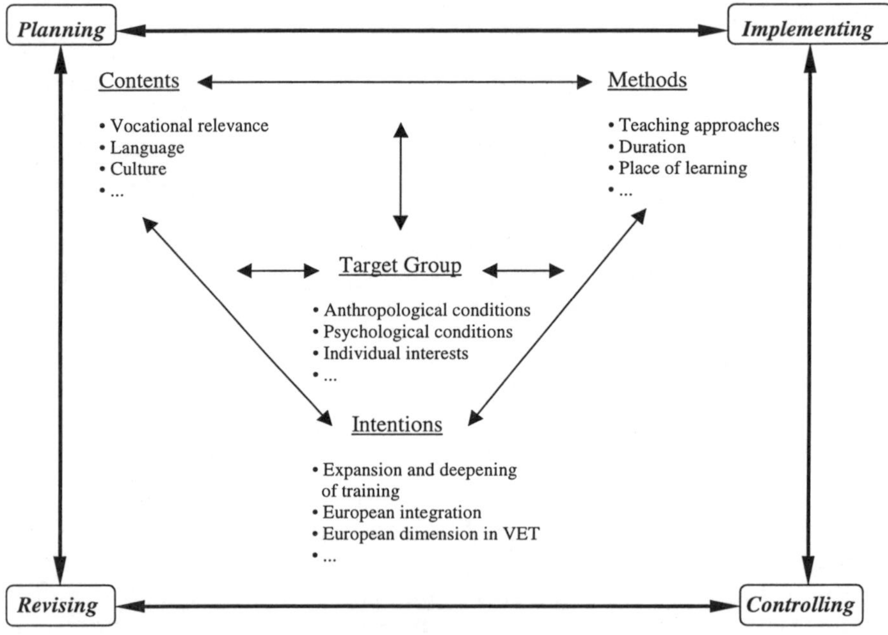

Figure 2. Didactic structure of European modules in vocational education and training.[74]

The elements of the inner part of the model (Contents, Methods, Intentions, Target Group) are the micro-didactic decision parameters and must be seen in close relation to each other: the choice of a certain intention of the module (e.g. to strengthen the European dimension of training) will inevitably influence the choice of the method of teaching (subject-specific vs cross-subject teaching), and so on. The central position of the target group emphasises the decisive influence of the individual potentials of trainees on the three other decision parameters. For example, German trainees with university entrance examinations (*Abitur*) do not normally require the teaching of basic English.[75] The four outer elements of the model refer to the dynamic character of modules: they are planned, implemented, controlled and revised in a constantly ongoing process to achieve the adaptation of the modules to the needs of the national training system (*cooperation level I*) and the individual training company (*cooperation level II*).

This model was used to design the modules of additional qualifications for the training of assistants in German craft professions as described in chapter 3 (Braukmann & Sloane, 1994).[76] Its transnational relevance is established as soon as the design process involves the two levels of cooperation introduced earlier. The model stresses the national systems of training as the starting-point of processes introducing a European perspective and the cooperation of practitioners as the basis for the creation of joint modules. This manner of developing and introducing European modules takes the specific philosophies of national systems of education and training into account; convergence could be achieved gradually. However, the assessment of the potential of this approach to overcome the extensive difficulties in developing and implementing European modules, as occurred in the EU Euroqualifications project (Sellin, 1994b, p. 9), remains a subject for further empirical research to assess.

CHAPTER 5

The Concept of Modularisation in NVQs and GNVQs

The Development of the Modularisation Approach in the United Kingdom

The development of modular structures in VET in England and Wales must be seen in the wider perspective of the great debate in education following Prime Minister James Callaghan's speech at Ruskin College, Oxford, in 1976. In the compulsory education sector, Callaghan's demands and the subsequent discussions led the way to the creation of a national curriculum for all pupils aged between 5 and 16, prescribed in the 1988 Education Reform Act. Furthermore, extending his criticism to the post-compulsory sector, Callaghan expressed his dissatisfaction with young people's preparation for the world of work.[77] He identified:

> *complaints from industry that new recruits from the schools sometimes do not have the basic tools to do the job that is required.*

He went on to express the concern:

> *that many of our best trained students who have completed the higher levels of education at university or polytechnic have no desire to join industry. (Callaghan, 1976)*

In the following years, the role of education as a means of improving economic competitiveness was widely discussed. This 'vocationalisation' of or 'new vocationalism' in education has been identified as a worldwide tendency at that time (Lauglo & Lillis, 1988; Cantor, 1989; Georg, 1997) and may be regarded as 'the end of the liberal consensus and the reassertion of the economic and vocational function of education' (Hyland, 1994a, p. 3; see also Coffey, 1992, ch. 5).[78]

The provisions for VET were trapped in a situation described later by Finegold & Soskice as the 'low-skills equilibrium in Britain', consisting of:

- a low participation in education after the compulsory school age;
- a lack of substantive policies to remedy the vacuum in training in the majority of companies; and
- a lack of measures to react to the changing skills needed to compete in a rapidly restructuring world economy (see Finegold & Soskice, 1988, p. 49ff.; Finegold et al, 1990, pp. 10–19).[79]

The traditional apprenticeship model in Britain was – contrary to its successful German counterpart and despite their common roots in the medieval craft guilds (see chapter 2) – closely related to certain declining sections of the manufacturing and construction industries. From the mid-1970s onwards, apprenticeships dramatically declined as those industries moved into recession. Therefore, it was assumed that the traditional apprenticeship system could not provide the framework to overcome the low-skills equilibrium.[80] Consequently, the Manpower Services Commission ([MSC] 1981, p. 4) set the 'modernisation of traditional apprenticeships' as one of the key goals for the reorganisation of training in Britain.

The MSC was created by the Conservative Government in 1973 and became the most important agent of planning and monitoring the developments in VET at the end of the 1970s (Raggatt & Unwin, 1991, p. xi; Franklin, 1997, p. 512ff.) Its broad goal was the development of a flexible and adaptable workforce through a more comprehensive strategy for manpower and skill development. Central to this goal was a system of vocational qualifications based on relevant standards of competence for all skilled occupations. Due to rapidly rising youth unemployment, the process of defining occupational standards gathered pace and was mirrored in the 1981 White Paper, *New Training Initiative: a programme for action*, which was endorsed by the Employment Department ([ED] 1981). The Initiative followed the recommendation of the MSC. Operationalised and implemented by the MSC, the standards formed the crucial basis for the assessment criteria of workplace training in the *Youth Training Scheme* (YTS) [81] (Jessup, 1985, pp. 166–170; Jessup, 1991, p. 150). Unlike the Technical and Vocational Initiative (TVEI) project of 1982 (Taylor, 1993) and the Certificate of Prevocational Education (CPVE), introduced in 1985 (Coffey, 1992, p. 171ff.), YTS (later labelled Youth Training – YT) assessed the achievements of the trainee against clearly defined 'standard tasks' (then grouped in 1984 into 'modules of accreditation') that provided a precise statement of the criteria for the successful performance of the task. These were presented in the form of outcomes rather than learning processes (MSC, 1984, p. 32). This type of provision, which was to be developed and defined in several programmes in the following years, most prominently in NVQs, is often referred to as 'competency-based education and training' (CBET).

In addition to the principles of occupational standards and outcome-based assessment, YTS was characterised by its modular structure. A module in this context was defined as a 'group of related skills and knowledge which forms a recognizable block of activity within an occupation or a subject' (Jessup, 1985, p. 171). As Young (1995, pp. 169–171) argues, in the United Kingdom, modularisation in VET developed primarily as a result of localised teacher initiatives in the early 1980s, like those supported by TVEI.[82] Nevertheless, the adoption of government policies centred upon competency-based strategies, like YTS, has provided the impetus for the development and implementation of modular courses on a national scale.[83] Although 'the New Training Initiative does not specifically refer to a modular structure for accreditation and training' (Jessup, 1985, p. 170), the outcome approach and modularisation seemed to be inextricably linked in all major programmes for VET initiated by the central government throughout the 1980s and the 1990s.[84] As the most prominent examples, NVQs and GNVQs follow modular approaches. Alongside these national qualifications, private providers of education and training like the Business and Technology Education Council (BTEC) [85], City and Guilds of London Institute (C & G) and Royal Society of Arts (RSA) follow their own modular strategies. Despite the Government's aim to incorporate all programmes from these providers into the NVQ framework, there is no legal obligation for them to integrate their programmes. Interestingly, many of these traditional qualifications have a high reputation and persistence in local markets, where they are accepted and demanded by both young people and employers (Stanyer, 1997, p. 54).

It is important to relate these developments in VET to the different types of modularity in existence within various qualifications and courses throughout the educational system in the United Kingdom. In the sector of higher education, Otter (1996, p. 31) describes the modularisation of undergraduate degree courses at British universities and argues that '"Going modular" became one of the major preoccupations of the late 1980s and early 1990s'. For the last 30 years, credit transfer arrangements have been extensively developed by the Open University (Richardson et al, 1995a, p. 32). Since the mid-1980s, different forms of modularised courses and assessment practices have been developed in the General Certificate of Secondary Education (GCSE), A levels and the more recently introduced AS levels. These developments in the school sector were aimed at overcoming subject barriers and the academic/vocational divide.[86]

In further education, the emphasis of colleges seems to be on unitisation of assessment procedures to facilitate credit accumulation and part-time study of adult students. Since the beginning of the 1990s, the Further Education Unit (FEU) has been developing the idea of a credit framework, the Credit Accumulation and Transfer (CAT) system for further education. Its purpose may be broadly described as the creation of a single frame of reference for learning within existing qualifications.[87] The CREDIS project in Wales has similar objectives for the integration of academic qualifications (GCSEs, A level) and qualifications in vocational training and further education (NVQs and GNVQs) (Stanyer, 1997, p. 50ff.) Finegold et al (1990) have even put forward the idea of an 'Advanced Diploma' for the whole age group between 16 and 19 years which would replace the current division between the vocational and academic tracks and include the higher education sector. They suggest individually credited modules as the main means of linkage between stages and institutions.[88]

Generally, in all of these sectors of education different approaches towards modularity and credit have flourished locally and resulted in a vast number of different initiatives, despite the relatively rigid national regulations introduced by and after the 1988 Education Reform Act.[89]

It was not until the mid-1990s that the policy of the Schools Curriculum and Assessment Authority (SCAA) started to hinder the application of modular principles by limiting the proportion of coursework assessment in GCSEs and A/AS levels. The National Council for Vocational Qualifications (NCVQ), on the other hand, encourages the development of modular provisions based on the assessment of learning outcomes. However, the public debate about these provisions in the NVQ framework mostly concentrates on the competence- and outcome-based approach of assessment and training [90], and does not focus on modularity.

The Modern Apprenticeship Scheme, announced during Britain's 1993 Autumn Budget, builds on some of the main features of the traditional apprenticeship model and is, therefore, less focused on outcomes than NVQs. Nevertheless, Modern Apprenticeships are closely bound to the NVQ model as they incorporate NVQ modules of certain levels into their provisions (cf. Richardson, 1998; Ertl, 1998b).

The different interests in the various educational sectors have produced a variety of different approaches towards modularisation. From the beginning of the 1980s, these approaches have developed as:

- a *reactive* approach for specific weaknesses (e.g. low attainment, lack of flexibility, detrimental effects of the academic/vocational divide);
- a *responsive* approach to system changes (e.g. increased participation in education after 16, changing qualification needs of industry and commerce); and
- a more *proactive* approach to future curriculum and qualification needs (e.g. to anticipate increased flexibility and mobility of labour, higher personal aspirations, consequences of lifelong learning).

The major temporal developments in restructuring and modularisation of educational provisions in England and Wales may be summarised as shown in Table VI.

Early 1980s

Ad hoc expansion of VET (YTS, TVEI, CPVE) and incremental pre-vocational and academic developments

Development of vocational qualifications based on units of learning (e.g. in YTS)

Mid-1980s

Establishment of a national framework for vocational qualifications (NVQs)

Development of modular structures in academic qualifications (GCSEs, A/AS levels)

Local specifications of units and credits in YTS programmes

Late 1980s

Education Reform Act, introduction of Training and Enterprise Councils (TECs), first NVQs and GCSEs awarded

Designs for a common core of learning in A levels and BTEC national qualifications

Development of competence- and outcomes-based units in NVQs

Design of core skills in BTEC National Awards

Early 1990s

Establishment of a national triple-track framework for all qualifications consisting of an academic (GCSEs, A/AS levels, degrees), a pre-vocational (GNVQs) and a vocational (NVQs) track

Development of various forms of credit frameworks in further education (e.g. CAT, CREDIS)

Development of GNVQs as modularised group awards

Proposals for developing a unified qualification framework for 16–19 year-olds on a modular basis (e.g. Advanced Diploma, National Certificate)

Mid-1990s

Introduction of Modern Apprenticeships

Review of the national framework (Dearing, Beaumont, Capey Reviews) and developing links between the tracks

Restrictions on modular A/AS levels

Alignment of A level and GNVQ structures

Roman type stipulates the main developments in restructuring;
Italic type gives the main developments in modularisation.

Table VI. Developments of restructuring and modularisation in education in England and Wales.[91]

Modularisation in NVQs

Implementation and Objectives

The NCVQ [92], established in 1986 as a result of the *Review of Vocational Qualifications* chaired by Oscar de Ville, tried to convert the traditional 'jungle of certificates' (Prais, 1989, p. 52) into a consistent system of nationally acknowledged qualifications in the field of VET.[93] Furthermore, the creation of a transparent framework of marketable vocational certificates was intended to enhance the status of vocational education, which was considered second-rate compared to the academic route. The new approach taken by the NCVQ can also be regarded as a reaction to the deficits and failures of YTS.[94] NVQs were designed as a framework for vocational qualifications comprehensively covering all occupations and professions (Jessup, 1995, p. 35).[95] The framework allocates qualifications to five levels spanning from training for operative activities to preparation for junior and senior management. For the definition of NVQ levels, see appendix VI, Table AI.

Institutional Framework of Standard Setting and Quality Assurance

In the NVQ model, the qualifications are formed by a specified number of learning units which correspond closely to the skills and knowledge required for a certain occupation. The institutional framework of the standard setting process is illustrated in Figure 3.

About 160 Industry Lead Bodies, which can be statutory training authorities, employer organisations or professional bodies, are recognised and partly funded by the Department for Education and Employment (DfEE). The Lead Bodies have the authority to define occupational standards (consisting of elements of competence, performance criteria and range statements) in an occupational area. In many cases, Lead Bodies establish Occupational Standards Councils within each occupational area to provide greater coherence in the provision of standards and the resulting qualifications. The vocational qualifications are the result of grouping sets of occupational standards into units of competence by selecting those relevant to particular work profiles. Alongside the qualifications, there is an assessment system, which is supposed to be capable of providing valid, reliable and cost-effective evidence that the standards have been achieved (cf. NCVQ, 1995, pp. 28–33, 40–45).

The complete qualification (the standards plus the assessment process) is then submitted to the Qualifications and Curriculum Authority (QCA), which took over the responsibilities of the NCVQ, for accreditation. If the qualification meets a number of criteria concerned with structure, relevance, coherence and access, it is accredited as an NVQ at one of the five levels. The QCA does not award or administer the qualification – this is done by over 110 separate Awarding Bodies (e.g. EDEXCEL, RSA, C & G). They use the standards and assessment processes to develop new learning programmes or to incorporate them into existing programmes which directly address the requirements defined by the qualification. It is also possible that the standards and assessment requirements are directly used by companies and other organisations to contribute to human resource development and management. The use of the standards and the qualifications is voluntary; therefore training providers and employers are free to ignore them or to use them to inform learning design without direct reference to NVQs. Awarding Bodies issue certificates for candidates achieving a full NVQ, and also certificates of unit credits for those achieving one or more NVQ units.

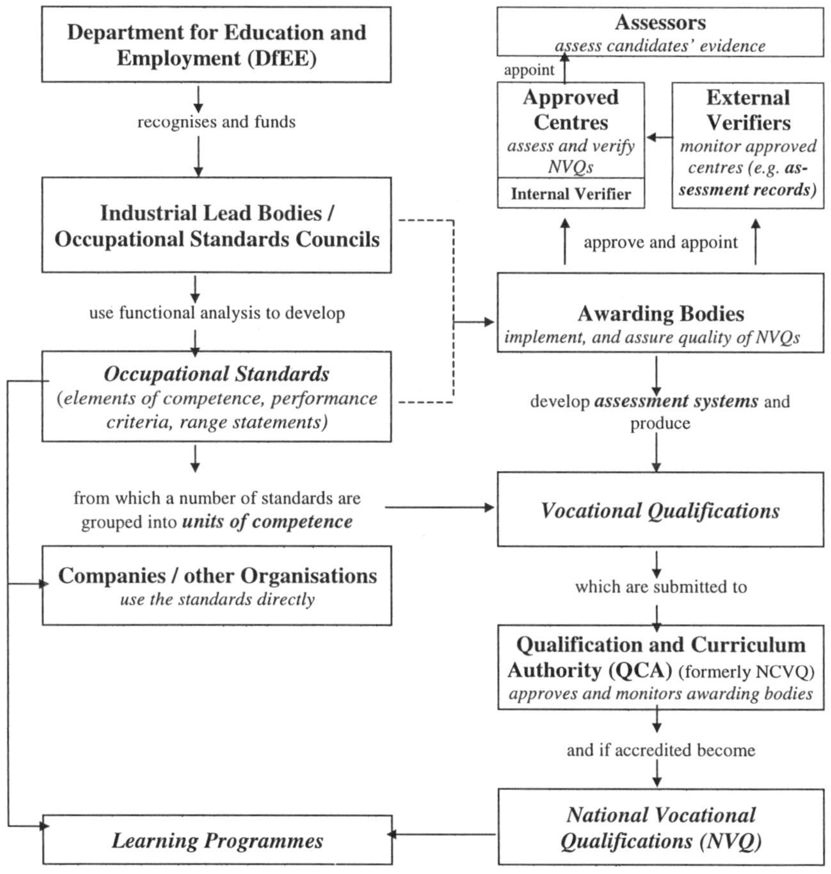

Figure 3. Institutional framework of NVQ standard setting and quality assurance.[96]

Following the *Awarding Bodies' Common Accord*, published in August 1997, strengthened assessment and verification procedures have come into action (QCA, 1997c, p. 7; cf. also NCVQ, 1995, pp. 40–45). Under these procedures, Approved Centres are responsible for delivering assessment on a day-to-day basis. They must have effective internal procedures to ensure the quality and consistency of assessment. Internal verifiers are responsible for advising assessors (appointed by Centres and assessing candidates' evidence) and for maintaining the quality of assessment in the Centre. Awarding Bodies, who approve the Centres, are responsible for verifying that assessment in a centre has been carried out systematically, has validity, and is up to national standards. This is achieved by external verifiers appointed by the Awarding Body. They act as the main link between Awarding Bodies and Centres and sample NVQ assessments in order to determine how well a Centre's internal quality control arrangements are operating. The external verifier requires access to full information about the Centre's activities in order to reach appropriate judgements. Thus, Centres must maintain records of all candidates undergoing assessment. These assessment records show the progress and achievements of candidates in NVQs and units.

Outcome Orientation and Unitisation

The outcome-oriented character of NVQs becomes clear if one keeps the definition of an NVQ 'as a *statement of competence* clearly relevant to work' in mind (Jessup, 1991, p. 15, author's italics). A statement of competence is formulated at the following levels of detail [97]:

- NVQ title;
- units of competence; and
- elements of competence, with associated performance criteria and range statements.

An element of competence and its associated performance criteria and range statements are also referred to collectively as *occupational standards* which – as mentioned earlier – are developed by the Lead Bodies.

This common format of statements of competence may be illustrated as shown in Figure 4.

In this context, the components of occupational standards have the following functions and features [98]:

- *Elements of competence* are the smallest and most detailed descriptions of outcomes in the NVQ system. Nevertheless, they should not be detailed so that they relate only to a specific task or job, employer or organisation.
- *Performance criteria* set out what must be achieved for the successful performance of the element of competence. They should refer to

successful outcomes of performance, not the procedures for carrying out the activity. The assessment systems of Awarding Bodies have to take these criteria into account. Assessment is regarded as the process of collecting evidence and making judgement on whether the performance criteria of each element of competence have been met.

- *Range statements* indicate the range of application of an element of competence. They ensure that elements are demonstrated and assessed in different contexts and, therefore, that skills and knowledge can be transferred from one situation to another. The boundaries set for the application of elements can be broad or narrow depending on the occupation. Range statements are also useful in providing guidelines as to what needs to be covered in programmes of learning and what needs to be assessed.

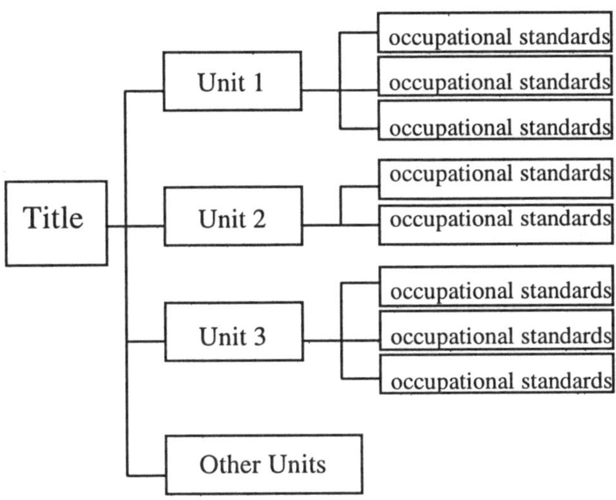

Figure 4. Format of the *Statement of Competence* of NVQs.[99]

All three components have a distinct semantic structure to make them more accessible.[100] The concept of range is used to provide a context for the occupational standards for the explicit purpose of assessment by setting the domain of the standard. The relationship between the three components of occupational standards may be illustrated as shown in Figure 5.

Furthermore, each element of competence has to be accompanied by:

- *knowledge specifications* (which describe what knowledge and understanding is considered necessary); and

- *evidence requirements* (which describe the minimum performance evidence acceptable, the quantity of particular types of evidence and evidence gathering methods).

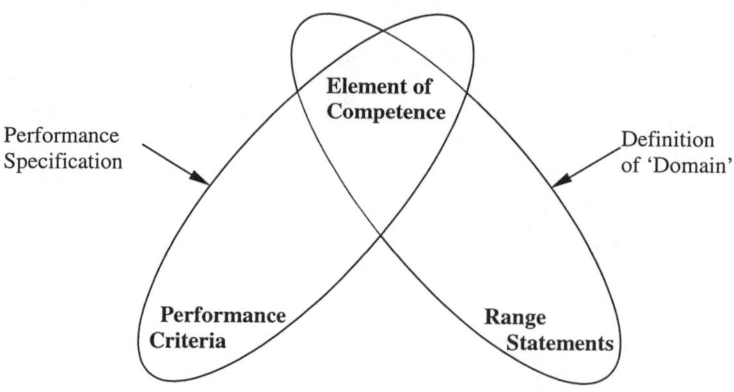

Figure 5. Specification and domain of occupational standards.[101]

Both represent mandatory parts of the specification of an NVQ and are provided by the Lead Body to facilitate the identification of evidence in the assessment process. This structure is valid for the three types of occupational units in NVQs: *mandatory*, *optional* and *additional* units. Whereas the mandatory units form the major part and train for the fundamental competences of an NVQ, optional and additional units provide trainees with opportunities for choice and specialisation.[102] The format of *core skill units* (in Communication, Application of Number, Information Technology, Personal Skills and Problem Solving) parallels that of occupational units and aims to enhance transferable skills across a broad spectrum of occupational areas. Lead Bodies are encouraged to develop core skill units for all occupations in their field but these units are not yet mandatory for all NVQs even though they are for GNVQs.

One or more elements of competence and the associated performance criteria and range statements form a *unit of competence*.[103] These are part-qualifications and are independently recognised and certificated. This structure provides a considerable degree of flexibility to the way in which NVQs can be built up through credit accumulation over time and in different locations. The elements of competence are grouped together so that the resulting unit corresponds to work functions.[104] The unit structure provides scope for rationalisation within the NVQ framework, as many functions are common to many occupations so that unit provisions can be shared (*common units*). If designed to the right size, units provide useful targets for trainees to aim at during the course of building up the competence required for a full NVQ. One or more units without a full qualification are certificated by the Awarding Bodies and can be used for credit accumulation in the National Record of Achievement (NRA).[105]

The way in which units are grouped to form an overall vocational qualification is similar to the way in which elements are grouped into units. The ability to perform a range of related activities that correspond to a work role is the general criterion for the selection of units for a specific NVQ. From the beginning of the 1990s onwards, the practical design process has shifted to the identification of employment functions that are then divided and subdivided into subfunctions and smaller functional elements. The results are functional maps which represent an entire occupational sector in terms of outcomes. Translated into elements of competence, these maps can be used as a basis for the design of qualifications. This process of *functional analysis* emphasises, in contrast to the formerly implied *task analysis* approach, the outcome orientation of NVQs as the purpose of work roles (functions) are at the start of the entire design process.[106]

Principles of Access, Learning and Assessment

NVQs have not been adopted as the basis of training provision for young people in the United Kingdom. Although they can contribute to the provision of learning for young people, they are not explicitly designed for this purpose. They are designed to open access to learning to the majority of the workforce irrespective of age. To achieve this, the statement of competence is independent of any course or training programme. Competences can be acquired through a variety of modes of learning, formal or informal, full-time or part-time, and in a variety of locations (cf. Jessup, 1991, p. 18ff.) To be assessed for a qualification, it is not necessary to have previously spent a specified period of time in education, training or the workplace. This principle marks a distinct difference from the tradition of apprenticeships in which entry is limited to a particular age, and the qualification is only achieved after specified modes and periods of training. Therefore, the NVQ model controls and regulates the outcomes of training and not the learning processes involved.

In some occupational areas, the workplace may be the only place where skills can be practised and acquired. In such cases, NVQs promote assessment in real-life situations at the workplace [107]:

> *performance must be demonstrated and assessed under conditions which allow accurate assessment of competence to the standard expected in employment – with evidence preferably derived from the workplace. (NCVQ, 1995, p. 29)*

For people without access to an appropriate workplace, simulations of the main work requirements in colleges and training workshops are promoted. The objective of open access is also the reason for allowing different kinds of evidence to be presented for assessment, as long as this evidence shows that the outcomes specified in the statements of competence are attained. This outcome-based assessment takes place continuously as the learning process unfolds, rather than in strict end-of-course examinations. Importantly, all outcomes are assessed, rather than just a sample. 'For an award of an NVQ a candidate must have demonstrated that he or she can meet the performance criteria of each element of competence specified' (NCVQ, 1989). However, NVQ criteria do not specify the specific method of assessment. Accreditation of prior learning (APL), including informal learning experiences, is also encouraged to facilitate the entry of people with work experience into the NVQ system (Jessup, 1991, ch. 8).

Concept of Modularisation

Considering the NVQ framework as a modularised system, the main characteristics seem to be its overall unitisation of the almost one thousand currently available qualifications (QCA, 1997b), the outcome orientation at the element and unit level, the variable order in which units can be accumulated without explicit time restrictions [108], its use of individual units in more than one qualification and its potentially high responsiveness to changing economic circumstances. These features would suggest that the NVQ falls into the fragmentation concept according to the concepts outlined in chapter 3. The main advantage of the fragmentation concept, namely, providing a highly flexible qualification framework, is potentially achieved by forming all qualifications from units, which are in turn formed by elements of competence, because units or even elements can be adapted without changing an entire qualification. By attaining optional or additional units, trainees can customise NVQs to their specific needs and interests.

However, the combination of units is limited, as NVQs are only awarded for certain combinations of units. Trainees are not entirely free to choose the units they regard as necessary for their needs.[109] The marketability of single units as part-qualifications is restricted, although there are certificates for single units that can be used for credit accumulation in the NRA. The NVQ as the full qualification, rather than single units, is the main objective of training. Therefore, some characteristics of the differentiation concept of modularisation are also valid for the NVQ model.

Modularisation in GNVQs

Implementation and Objectives

General National Qualifications (GNVQs) were first announced in the 1991 White Paper, *Education and Training for the 21st Century*; they were piloted in September 1992 and introduced in September 1993.[110] In the White Paper, the Government declared its intention of establishing 'parity of esteem' between academic and vocational education. The NCVQ was given the remit to extend the NVQ framework to include broad-based vocational qualifications that could be delivered through full-time programmes in schools and colleges. As a reaction to the ongoing criticism of narrowness faced by NVQs (e.g. expressed by Hyland, 1994b, p. 241), GNVQs are designed to contain a broad knowledge base. Therefore, students are required to attain certain numbers of vocational units *and* units in core skills.[111] Furthermore, they are concerned with the continuation of general education whilst having a definite vocational orientation. They aim to prepare for various occupations in a vocational area, not, like NVQs, for a specific work role.[112] GNVQs are intended as an alternative to A levels for those who want a more practical extension of their learning and thus are designed as an alternative to higher education.[113]

The number of units required depends on the envisaged level of GNVQ: foundation, intermediate or advanced level, each equivalent to other qualifications (e.g. the advanced level, the so-called 'vocational A level', is equivalent to two A levels or NVQ level 3). For a juxtaposition of GNVQ levels, required units and equivalent qualifications see appendix VI, Table AII.

The underlying objective is to encourage a far higher proportion of young people to stay in full-time education beyond compulsory schooling. GNVQs have been introduced to link academic and vocational systems. The relationship between NVQs, GNVQs and academic qualifications can be illustrated in a 'three-track' system for the 14–19 age group (Pring, 1995, p. 71; QCA, 1997b, p. 7). GNVQs Part One are pre-16 vocational courses that represent the link to the National Curriculum as they are taken over about 2 years of Key Stage 4.

However, the three-track system continues to be highly criticised for its lack of coherence and failure to incorporate the variety of training provisions already in place (Pring, 1995, pp. 70–73; Tomlinson, 1997, p.1ff.; Young & Spours, 1998, p. 90ff.) By the mid-1990s, over 50% of qualifications offered by further education colleges lay outside the three-track system; a clear indication that this system has not found sufficient acceptance with its main target group, which seems to be isolated and overtaxed in an 'unstable context for choices' (Butterfield, 1998, p. 9). For instance, the aim of GNVQs to develop a link to academic qualifications by providing the opportunity for students to opt for

A levels or GCSEs instead of additional vocational units appears not to have materialised (Spours, 1995b, p. 19).

Institutional Framework of Standard Setting and Quality Assurance

GNVQs are awarded by EDEXCEL, C & G and the RSA. Their function as Awarding Bodies in relation to the QCA is similar to the structure of the NVQ framework.[114] The QCA is responsible for overseeing the development of GNVQs and ensuring that national standards are maintained. The mandatory units of GNVQs are devised centrally (like NVQ occupational standards); optional and additional units are developed by the Awarding Bodies. The Awarding Bodies approve schools, colleges or other institutions as GNVQ Centres which deliver GNVQs. The requirements for approval include criteria for quality control management and administration systems, delivery of provisions, physical and staff resources, and so on. The QCA develops the standards of GNVQs in cooperation with the Awarding Bodies. In contrast to NVQs, the contents and levels of the envisaged outcomes, which form the qualification, are specified without the influence of industry.[115]

The quality assurance measures are derived from the NVQ framework described earlier. Nevertheless, there are some important differences. Schools and colleges vary considerably in terms of the nature of their local economy and resources. GNVQs recognise these variations and allow flexibility to make best use of local circumstances. However, national standards through the specification of outcomes, partly through approaches derived from NVQs, ensure that standards are maintained. GNVQ teachers not only plan and deliver programmes of learning but also design the internal assessment process.[116] To fulfil this function they are required to become qualified assessors by acquiring centrally prescribed qualifications. Internal verifiers appointed in each school or college monitor the teachers. An external verifier who visits Centres to check the assessment practice must confirm the quality of assessment.[117] In order to facilitate assessment and verification, students keep their work in *portfolios of evidence*. These portfolios are the basis of inspections by verifiers when they examine the quality of assessment. Students must take responsibility for organising and maintaining their portfolios and, therefore, for managing the outcomes of their own learning.

Outcome Orientation and Unitisation

The unitised structure of GNVQs corresponds to the NVQ model: *elements of achievement* (NVQ: elements of competence) and associated *performance criteria*, *range statements* and *evidence indicators* (NVQ: evidence requirements) are grouped into units which are in turn grouped into the full qualifications. Furthermore, *amplification and guidance* were added as new components to each element of achievement to clarify key terms and the depth of study required (BTEC, 1994, Part I, p. 16). For an example of the structure of an element of achievement, see appendix VIII.

As for NVQ units, GNVQ units are defined in terms of outcomes which the student must achieve. This structure is valid for all three kinds of GNVQ units (for details see appendix VI, Table AII):

- *mandatory vocational units:* cover skills and knowledge needed for a broad range of jobs in a chosen vocational area;
- *optional vocational units:* complement the mandatory units and give students an opportunity to specialise; and
- *core skill units:* develop skills in Communication, Application of Number, Information Technology (mandatory) and Working with Others, Problem Solving, Improving Own Learning and Performance (additional).

Students also have the opportunity to extend their achievement by taking additional GNVQ (vocational or core skill) units and additional studies. By achieving a merit or distinction award, students aiming for the advanced level improve their chances for university entrance. Individual units are not graded. The knowledge introduced in lower-level units underpins the knowledge in higher-level units even if the titles of units in a vocational area are not the same at the different levels. As a broad guideline, it can be stated that units have similar size at a given level; vocational units require about 60 hours of structured learning time.

As in NVQs, units in GNVQs can be assessed and certificated separately and are grouped into the full qualification. This allows credit accumulation throughout a course and credit transfer between qualifications. As assessment is based on units rather than on the full qualification, modular delivery is common practice. The crucial point to note is, however, that both GNVQ and NVQ units are units of assessment, not units of instruction. Whereas modular assessment is obligatory according to the NCVQ regulations, the style of instruction is a matter for Awarding Bodies to decide (Stanyer, 1997, p. 55). The translation of the curriculum into modules expressed as learning outcomes creates scope for the development of more student-centred approaches and individualised learning modes (Nasta, 1994, p. 83).

Principles of Access, Learning and Assessment

Owing to their outcome orientation, GNVQs are flexible concerning the learning activities of students. The appropriateness of different learning methods depends on the demands of individual units. Although various teaching methods can be found in practice, the emphasis of GNVQs on learners' activity often results in collaborative styles of learning. These were regarded as one of the benefits of GNVQs in the 1994 Office for Standards in Education inspection report ([OFSTED] 1994b, p. 5). The students' responsibility for their own learning is enhanced.[118] Following the NVQ model of outcomes, learning and assessment are separated in terms of classroom delivery (see Figure 6). As in NVQs, GNVQ students have to deliver evidence for all outcomes prescribed in the elements of achievement. The students are assessed by a combination of the following components [119]:

- continuous *internal assessment*, including integrated assessment of core skill units (assessment within the context of the chosen vocational area): students keep their assessed evidence of achievement in portfolios of evidence which are the basis for assessment;
- *external assessment* on three occasions a year for each mandatory vocational unit: Awarding Bodies set and mark tests which are produced alongside unit specifications; and
- *grading assessment*: to decide whether students have achieved a merit or distinction grade for the GNVQ award.

Priority is given to internal assessment, which runs throughout the GNVQ, because it is the only practical way in which the breadth of cognitive and vocational skills can be assessed. Evidence can be accumulated over weeks and months towards the achievement of an outcome. The GNVQ is awarded when evidence included in the student's portfolio meets all the requirements of the performance criteria for the required number of units (see appendix VI, Table AII) and the external tests have been passed. The selection function of the assessment process is fulfilled by what was described as a 'second order' grading system (Jessup, 1995, p. 47). This means the continuous review of students' work against specified criteria and not differentiation between students at a certain point in time. Students accumulate evidence for meeting the required standards. Although no formal entry requirements are specified for GNVQs, tutors are bound to ensure that all students accepted on a course can achieve the standard necessary for the award. The grading assessment for merit and distinction grades is made against additional standards. Assessment against predetermined standards is derived from the NVQ model and is in principle also valid for GNVQs. Figure 6 illustrates how both assessment and learning are based on predetermined outcomes in the form of standards of achievement (NVQ: standards of competence), but are conceptually independent of each other.

Concept of Modularisation

As described in the previous sections, the design of GNVQs is derived from the NVQ framework in most aspects. The unitised structure suggests that the GNVQ model, like the NVQ model, represents characteristics of the differentiation and the fragmentation concept of modularisation (as defined in chapter 3).

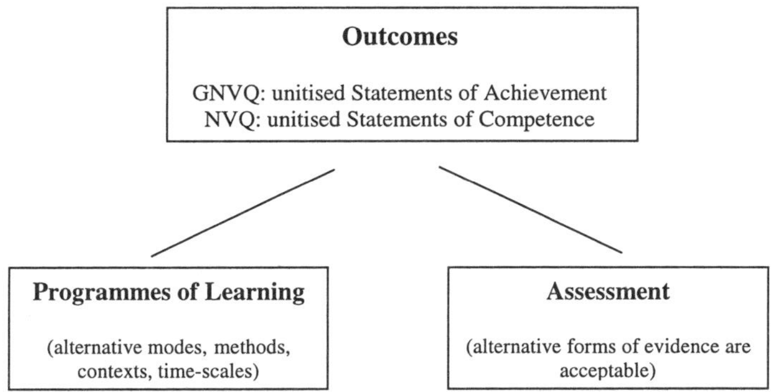

Figure 6. NVQ/GNVQ curriculum model.[120]

However, in marked contrast to modular syllabuses, which in most cases have short-term goals, the assessment of GNVQs is focused on the application of grading criteria to evidence accumulated over substantial periods of time. GNVQs do not benefit from the advantage of a close link between learning and assessment in terms of feedback and planning, typical for modular structures. The learning tends to be organised in whole-year courses rather than a series of modules assessed cumulatively (Richardson et al, 1995a, p. 10). Spours (1995b, p. 17), therefore, argues, 'To call GNVQs a modular award is a misnomer. It is a unitised qualification that stresses an integrated method of delivery using NVQ-type performance criteria'. The emphasis of GNVQs on integrated methods of delivery must be seen in the tradition of pre-vocational education in the United Kingdom and is the major difference to the modular structure of NVQs. It has been argued that GNVQs can only be partially regarded as initial qualifications for the world of work and that they are only to a certain extent comparable to vocational qualifications in Germany (Stanyer, 1997, p. 56). Therefore, it is not surprising that it is difficult to classify GNVQs using the conceptualisations from chapter 3, which are explicitly derived from the vocational context in Germany.

A Critical Account of Modularisation in NVQs and GNVQs

In 1995, Sir Ron Dearing was given the remit to advise on how to 'strengthen, consolidate and improve the framework of 16 to 19 qualifications' (Dearing, 1996). The review took place in parallel with the Capey Review of GNVQs (Capey, 1995) and the Beaumont Review of NVQs (Beaumont, 1995). This can be regarded as an admission that the 'three-track' system of academic A levels, pre-vocational GNVQs and vocational NVQs, as proposed by the 1991 White Paper *Education and Training for the 21st Century*, showed substantial weaknesses (Stanton, 1997, p. 49).

The weaknesses of the whole system and the qualifications have been criticised extensively in the specialist educational literature as well as in the mass media.[121] It is impossible within the scope of this study to elaborate on all the strands of criticism that NVQs and GNVQs are facing. Therefore, the emphasis here lies on the main areas of criticism and in particular those criticisms which relate to the modular structure of these qualifications.

The numbers of students attempting both NVQs and GNVQs are not satisfactory. A study undertaken for the DfEE in 1997, aimed at assessing the factors which influence the take-up of NVQs and SVQs (Scottish Vocational Qualifications), concludes that 'the take-up of NVQs/SVQs is still low compared with other vocational qualifications and take-up is concentrated amongst certain groups of individuals' (Callendar, 1997, p. vii). Smithers (1997, p. 61ff.) shows how the officially reported numbers of awards and the actual numbers given in reality differ substantially. Indeed, if the number of completed qualifications is taken to be the relevant indicator of the NVQ model's success, it must be stressed that the targeted 50% of the workforce who were envisaged to be trained for NVQs or GNVQs has not been reached. Two-thirds of the vocational qualifications currently awarded are the old-style pre-NVQ awards. GNVQs show pass rates of only about 40% and, similar to NVQs, completed awards are centred in a few occupational areas. A large proportion of employers seems to be indifferent to or ignorant of the nature and purposes of both qualifications (Spilsbury et al, 1995, p. 2ff.; Hyland, 1996, p. 350). The aim of the NVQ framework to provide a basis for most post-compulsory vocational awards has not been achieved. Critics argue that the disappointing take-up and completion rates are the result of conceptual rather than technical problems, as was argued in the Beaumont Review (1995, p. 34).

First, in the NVQ model, the concepts of knowledge and understanding are based on the instrumental application of knowledge rather than theoretical and investigative enquiry. A reservoir of theoretical knowledge and understanding, essential for a flexible workforce, is not provided. Therefore, the competences credited in NVQs 'only reveal people's ability to deal with yesterday's problems, but leave people helpless when faced with tomorrow's' (Sparkes, 1994). The tendency towards an insufficient knowledge base for a changing working world is further exaggerated by the unitised structure of both NVQs and GNVQs. Meeting criteria based on specifications of units, performance criteria and range statements tends to fragment understanding (Smithers, 1995). There is no guarantee that even a high number of elements of competence (GNVQ: elements of achievement) derived from functional analysis will amount to skilled overall performance. The orientation of qualifications towards specific work role functions, and the division of these functions into pedagogically unconnected units, leads to fragmented overall qualifications and disintegrated curricula (Braun, 1994, p. 29).[122] Complicated and costly assessment procedures are the results of an enormous amount of test criteria (Reuling, 1996, p. 51ff.; Smithers, 1997, p. 58ff.). In 1995, therefore, an attempt was made by the Joint Council of the Vocational Awarding Bodies and the NCVQ 'to reduce the burden on teachers and students, making assessment and grading [of GNVQs] more consistent' (Joint Council of the Vocational Awarding Bodies, 1995).

Bruijn & Howieson (1995, p. 95) and Cornford (1997, p. 238) argue that competency-based training in a modularised form would neglect cognitive psychology and learning theory as they are based on narrow behaviourist principles. This would lead to the fragmentation of related knowledge and consequently, such knowledge would only be applicable to one occupational task.[123] The assumption of the NVQ model that knowledge would be reflected by skilled performance is also problematic. This assumption is called into question by structuralist theories that relate performance to the existence of an underlying system of cognitive structures. According to the structuralist theory, competence is only achieved if an appropriate system of regulating cognitive structures has been developed to solve a problem, and not just if the performance of a person suggests that a problem can be solved (Heursen, 1983).[124]

CHAPTER 6

A Strategy of Modularisation in German Initial Training

As argued in the introduction and in chapter 2, modularisation in the German vocational education and training system is used in the areas of further training, retraining and in the qualification of adult workers. In the area of initial training, modular structures have only been tested in pilot schemes, for instance, in the provision of additional qualifications. In this concluding chapter, one possible strategy of modularisation for the German initial training sector is proposed based on the findings of the previous chapters. The strategy is limited to changes within the existing legislative framework as there is a consensus of the social partners that reform should take place without giving up the 'concept of the vocation' (cf. Pütz, 1997, p. 68). In this proposal, it is suggested that the strengths and potentials of the present system must be preserved, particularly with regard to its responsiveness and the flexibility of training provisions. The reasons for introducing modularisation into other European systems do not apply in the German case. In the Spanish and Scottish systems (and to a certain extent in England and Wales), modularisation was introduced to set up an overall training framework or coordinate an existing, insufficiently regulated one. However, this is not necessary in the German context as the provisions of the Dual System are well established and the training sector is already highly regulated (cf. Deissinger, 1996a, p. 191).

In the German instance then, the proposed strategy is to further develop the existing elements of occupational profiles (*Berufsbildpositionen*) into self-contained part-qualifications which fulfil the functions of modules.[125] At the moment, occupational profiles are divided into a number of elements regarded as relevant for a vocation. According to the envisaged characteristics of modules developed in chapter 3 (cf. Table III), these elements of occupational profiles and the current accreditation procedures have to be transformed in the following ways.

Development of outcome specifications. Up to the present day, the elements of occupational profiles primarily specify the training processes. They state a list of contents that form the basis for training frameworks and curricula. To fulfil the functions of modules, the elements additionally have to specify the competences at which the learning processes are aimed. This outcome orientation is necessary to ensure the integrative function of modules, i.e. that the outcomes of individual modules contribute to the aim of the overall qualification, namely, to give the trainee sufficient 'vocational competence' (cf. 'concept of the vocation', chapter 2). The current development of multilingual training profiles resulting from the need for more transparent vocational certificates in the Single European Market is regarded as a first step to supplement German provisions with outcome criteria (Benner, 1997b; Herz & Jäger, 1998, p. 15). The development of the elements in the manner described in this chapter could avoid the pitfalls of the exclusive outcome orientation of modules, which is the source of severe criticism in the case of NVQs and GNVQs. By developing modules within the framework of existing recognised training occupations, the danger of fragmentation in the VET sector, one of the main criticisms faced by NVQs and GNVQs (Smithers, 1997, p. 57), can be minimised.

The proposed strategy designs 'skill focus' modules rather than 'system focus' modules (Bruijn & Howieson, 1995, p. 90). The modularisation in the Dutch printing industry, described in Table V and appendix IV, is an example of this kind of design process. Furthermore, the strategy follows the well-accepted approach of quality control in German VET by a combination of input and output regulation (Reuling, 1997, p. 64ff.), and is, therefore, compatible with the overall German regulatory framework.

Development of an adequate accreditation instrument. If the elements of occupational profiles are transferred into self-contained modules, then a means to accredit them individually is necessary. The only means of ensuring that the standards of the part-qualifications are comparable and that the combination of the modules into an overall qualification is unambiguous is by certifying the elements (or modules) in a widely accepted way. Yet again, developments resulting from processes at a European level provide valuable hints as to what such an accreditation instrument could look like.

The long-standing demand for a 'passport of vocational education' (*Berufsbildungspaß*) accepted Europe-wide reflects the need for a recognised instrument of accreditation of part-qualifications to ensure comparability of vocational certificates within the EU. As described in chapter 3, this instrument could facilitate the continuation of training in such a case as that of an overall qualification not being achieved at the first attempt.[126] The frequently criticised 'all-or-nothing character' of the German Dual System, which is focused on the all-decisive final examination, could be toned down by the accreditation of modules as part-qualifications during the training process. The British experiences with the National Record of Achievement can provide valuable suggestions concerning the establishment of a similar record in Germany and Europe. The development of the CREDIS project in Wales (cf. chapter 5) is an interesting example of how such a 'passport' could function as the link between initial and further training qualifications as well as between the vocational and the general education sector. It remains to be seen whether the EUROPASS training (introduced in January 2000) can be further developed and if it will eventually assume the functions required for accrediting training modules.

Development of modular assessment systems. Closely linked to the question of accreditation is the issue of assessment of part-qualifications. As the legislative foundation of the Dual System, in particular the Vocational Training Act of 1969, does not provide for such a system, the experiences of pilot projects in Germany and of practice abroad need to be drawn upon when developing assessment procedures for elements of occupational profiles. In particular, the issues of who assesses and how assessment is conducted have to be addressed.

It is suggested by critics of NVQs and GNVQs that there is a danger of overregulating the assessment procedures, which leads to complicated and costly testing regimes (Reuling, 1996, p. 51ff.; Smithers, 1997, p. 58ff.) The experiences of German pilot schemes introducing modular structures to the further training and retraining sector suggest that there are different modes of assessment conceivable (Davids, 1996; Collingro & Dellbrück, 1997; Kunkel & Paluch, 1997; Weinhuber, 1997; Herz & Jäger, 1998). In general, it can be concluded that the training company has to be given the responsibility for assessment and for the choice of the appropriate testing method. It is important that the testing method and the acquired competences are described in the trainees' 'passports'. The assessment of individual modules cannot replace the final examination for the overall qualification, which remains essential for the acceptance of vocational certificates in Germany. Problems with the marketability of NVQs and GNVQs show that the well-established character of vocational qualifications in Germany (Deissinger, 1996b, p. 200) should not be compromised by omitting one of the main factors for their widespread acceptance, the rigorous final examinations. This does not exclude the adaptation of the concept of final examinations arising from new demands in a modernised qualification system (cf. the proposals by Syfried, 1997).

Development of modules with multiple relevance. Currently, the elements of the occupational profiles are specifically developed for each of about 370 recognised training occupations. In a modular structure, the design process of elements has to be conducted with the aim of making them relevant for more than one occupational area. As described in chapter 3, the sharing of modules is a major potential of modularity in VET to increase the economic efficiency of provisions. The didactic structure of 'European modules' as described in the model in chapter 4 can be a guideline for the design process of modules relevant to several areas of occupation. Significantly, the design process has to take place within the corporative structure of the German regulatory framework to ensure that employers and unions of the different occupational areas generally accept the standards of the modules. Sloane (1997a, p. 237ff.) argues that new organisational structures for the design process of modules still need to be developed as the existing structures were produced under very different circumstances and for substantially different purposes.

The strategy of modularisation proposed here harnesses the potentials of modularity in VET in several ways. In the classification of modular concepts, as suggested in chapter 3 (cf. Table IV), the strategy represents the differentiation concept as it restructures existing overall qualifications. The combination of self-contained modules (i.e. further developed and redesigned elements of occupational profiles) is regulated by an overall qualification, and modules are generally only marketable as part of such a qualification. The introduction of a 'passport of vocational education' as an instrument to accredit individual modules and some of the positive effects of the expansion concept of modularisation (cf. Table IV) play a role in the process of integrating initial and further training. The main advantages of the proposed strategy may be summarised as follows [127].

- *Increased responsiveness of provisions to changing economic and social environments.* The reform or adaptation of individual modules, instead of an entire overall qualification, reduces the time and costs of responsiveness. The development of optional modules can respond to the training needs of individual companies or collectively respond to the companies within a specific regional or occupational area.
- *Clear-cut value of part-qualifications in a more intelligible system.* The accreditation of modules in a 'passport of vocational education' offers better opportunities for the accreditation of prior learning, for retraining and for acquiring overall initial qualifications at a later career stage. In a European context, such a passport can increase the comparability of vocational qualifications. The integration of 'European modules' into national provisions can be a starting point for a coherent VET system at a European level.

- *Individualised and flexible provisions by offering additional and remedial modules.* High-achieving trainees can acquire part-qualifications during their time of initial training, which are currently unavailable to them, such as those which belonged to the sector of further training or to other occupational profiles. Remedial modules can foster disadvantaged trainees.[128] Individual pathways of qualification and flexible training periods are possible.

Undoubtedly, the proposed strategy needs to be refined in the light of further findings from international comparisons and the analysis of foreign experiences, including the future developments of modular approaches abroad. Pütz (1997, pp. 63, 74) even argues that modularisation cannot be a determining issue in the debate about the modernisation of VET in Germany at the moment because he considers the research basis insufficient. Whether or not one agrees with this stance, certainly the developments in England and Wales have to be taken into account, as they deal with many processes within the economic environment which are similar to the German context. However, it is also necessary to consider experiences with modularity in other European countries, since to concentrate on developments in England and Wales could be misleading due to the fundamental differences in the tradition of VET in England and Wales in comparison with Germany. For the development of a coherent training system at a European level, modularity in national provisions can be helpful in establishing links between what can be in many cases very diverse systems. Importantly, the different ideas in European countries about the function of training in society and the different attitudes towards concepts of vocations and occupations have to be taken into account (Sloane, 1993, p. 117; Münk, 1997, p. 6). Modularisation in EU countries certainly cannot be prescribed by a central institution but must build on the particular social traditions and processes in the countries and regions. Gonon (1998, p. 306) argues, therefore, for an 'evolutionary' development of modularity on the basis of existing education and training systems. In the German context, this would mean that modularisation in the training sector has to build on the structures of the Dual System.

Undoubtedly, the strategy proposed here, to further develop the existing elements of occupational profiles into modules, is one possible mechanism for such an evolutionary development. It cannot solve, and is not intended as an answer to, all questions concerning a modernised training system in Germany in the future. In particular, the role of the vocational schools in a modular structure seems to be unclear. The cooperative process of coordination between the two major learning venues in the Dual System, the training company and the vocational schools, which is perceived as difficult and demanding under the current provisions (Pätzold, 1997), would result in more challenges for the trainers and teachers concerned. This would be even more true if the Dual System was to be extended to a 'Plural System' (Kutscha, 1993, p. 49) which formally incorporates institutions like external training centres and polytechnics into a modularised training framework.[129] Furthermore, the relationship between VET and other areas in the educational system needs to be redefined.[130]

However, the strategy described here is firmly based within the structures that have developed over the long history of the Dual System, whilst also taking the changing economic and sociocultural conditions into account (Rützel, 1997, p. 7). By stressing the overall qualification as the integrative basis of individual modules, the danger of a degeneration of training to the mere preparation for a company-specific, short-term job (Sloane, 1993, p. 115) is minimised. The idea of initial training as a phase in the education and development of young people's personality remains central.

In this study, an attempt to clarify concepts like 'module' and 'modularisation' has been made as the concepts are used very ambiguously and vaguely in many cases. Further work on the conceptualisation of these terms certainly needs to be done in the future to ensure that the debate about modularity does not end in unhelpful language games (Orthey, 1998, p. 298ff.) This is even more the case at an international level. It must be considered that the educational terminology is embedded into the system of education it aims to describe, and which is in turn 'a living thing, the outcome of forgotten struggles and difficulties, and "of battles long ago"', as Michael Sadler (1900, p. 49) argued a century ago. The value of comparative education as a discipline can be used for the development of modularity in the German initial training system only if the different concepts of modularisation and modules and the traditions of the VET systems are the starting-point of cross-national comparisons. In this perspective, Harold Noah (1984, p. 158ff.) has concluded that the appropriate comparison of educational practices is as follows:

> *The authentic use of comparative study resides not in wholesale appropriation and propagation of foreign practices but in careful analysis of the conditions under which certain foreign practices deliver desirable results, followed by consideration of ways to adapt those practices to conditions found at home.*

Notes

[1] For example, Kloas (1997a, p. 18) suggests that controlling departments of companies may favour modularisation only because they hope to cut the costs of training. Others seem to use the term with inflationary frequency, because it sounds modern and progressive, without understanding the concept at all.

Hagedorn (1997, p. 18) characterises the trade unions' attitude towards modularisation in VET as a 'primeval fear' which is not objectively justified. For example, some unions believe their right to free collective bargaining is endangered by modularisation (Münk, 1997, p. 7).

[2] Examples for this rather superficial point of view are the reaction of the German Federal Government to the *Memorandum of the EU Commission for the Community's Policy in Vocational Education in the 1990s*: 'Modules as a regulatory framework are rejected' (quoted in Lipsmeier & Münk, 1994, p. 77ff.; Münk, 1995, p. 35); and the wholesale disapproval of certificates for modules by many employers because they would represent 'an inadequate alternative to the current vocational examinations' (quoted in Deissinger, 1996a, p. 190).

The first reactions against modularisation in Germany came from craft trades as the traditional apprenticeship system has a strong base within them (Zentralverband des Deutschen Handwerks, 1993; Cleve & Kell, 1996, p. 19).

[3] There is, inevitably, a certain level of selective perception, leading to an implicit comparison of the NVQ model with similar German structures, as the author's experiences are shaped by the German system.

[4] In this section, a brief overview of the historical development of vocational training is provided, restricted to that which is relevant to the present study. In particular, a short historical account seems to be necessary to enable the contemporary Dual System structures (as introduced in the next section) to be understood in the proper context (Groothoff, 1964, p. 21).

[5] The earliest known document referring to guild-regulated apprenticeship training is the ordinance of the Cologne wood turners dated 1182.

[6] Contrary to this legislation, the 'general certificate of competence' (*Großer Befähigungsnachweis*) of 1936 made the status of 'master craftsman' not only necessary for training apprentices but also for running a business.

The status of 'master craftsman', in turn, was regulated by the Chambers of Crafts, constituted in 1900 (Rothe, 1995, p. 79ff.)

[7] Deissinger (1992, pp. 404–412) identifies the reason for the decline of the English apprenticeship system during the twentieth century in the lack of coherence between the development of the educational system and the process of industrialisation from the end of the nineteenth century onwards. Whereas German industry regarded learning exclusively at industrial workplaces as insufficient to ensure comprehensive occupational qualifications, and therefore initiated training workshops for employees and developed industry-specific training, the English education and training system did not react to the new demands of industrial work structures. With the growth of industry, the decline of the crafts-based apprenticeship system was inevitable.

For a comparison of the developments of training provisions in England and Germany from the Industrial Revolution to the 1920s, see Deissinger (1994).

[8] Due to differing levels of industrialisation within German states and municipalities, industrial Sunday schools were structured in a variety of ways, and had differing spheres of influence (Neugebauer, 1992, p. 108ff.) In general it can be said that the typical German particularism (*Kleinstaaterei*) led to a vast diversity of legislative and institutional provisions at this time.

[9] Georg Kerschensteiner's prize essay on the 'Civic Education of the German Youth' of 1901 (*Staatsbürgerliche Erziehung der deutschen Jugend*, Preisschrift der Erfurter Akademie der Wissenschaft, in Simons, 1966) represented probably the most important step on the way from the '*Fortbildungsschule* to the *Berufsschule*' (Thyssen, 1954).

[10] For the political backgrounds of the Act, cf. Deissinger (1996b).

[11] This model must be seen in contrast to the *bureaucratic model* (the state alone plans, organises and controls vocational training) and the *market model* (the state plays no role, the provision of training is regulated solely by supply and demand). For other attempts to classify vocational training systems, see Greinert (1994, p. 11ff.)

[12] This *corporative* structure in vocational training can be traced back to the amendments to the Trade Code in 1897 and 1908 (Kutscha, 1998, p. 270).

The theory of *corporatism* proposes the organisation of the whole society into industrial and professional *corporations* serving as organs of political representation and exercising some control over persons and activities within their jurisdiction while still being subordinated to the state (cf. 'corporatism' in *Encyclopaedia Britannica* [1997]; Emile Durkheim's ideas on corporatism in: Aron [1967, p. 85ff.] and Wagner [1991, p. 230ff.])

[13] For details on VET in the former GDR, see Panorama (1985), European Centre for the Development of Vocational Education ([CEDEFOP] 1995, p. 32ff.), and Sloane (1997b).

[14] The identification of phases here summarises very briefly the periodisation of Greinert (1994, pp. 22–79). He employs the critical and functionalist approach developed by Offe (1975) to assess the developmental aspects of the vocational training sector as a social system. For the pitfalls of historical periodisation in comparative education in general, see Phillips (1994).

For alternative periodisation (not only of the Dual System but of German VET in general), see Lipsmeier (1978), Taylor (1981) and CEDEFOP (1995). For the development of vocational schools, see Abel (1963) and Thyssen (1954).

[15] This high participation rate establishes the Dual System as the regular framework for training in Germany. School-based programmes play a relatively minor role in numerical terms. Raggatt (1988, p. 166) calls the Dual System the 'centrepiece of vocational education and training in the Federal Republic'. For this reason, and because the debate on modularisation is concentrated on this dominating training sector, this study focuses on the Dual System.

For the complementary functions of the Dual System and school-based training in German VET, see Hahn (1997). For the latest numbers of newly concluded training contracts rates, see Bundesministerium für Bildung, Wissenschaft, Forschung und Technologie ([BMBF] 1998, p. 13ff.) For a comparison of figures in other countries, see Her Majesty's Inspectorate ([HMI] 1991, p. 31).

[16] The 'first threshold' hinders the transition from compulsory schooling to initial training (Deissinger, 1996b, p. 323).

[17] The publications dealing with the Dual System in English include Raggatt (1988), HMI (1991 and 1995), Federal Minister (1992), Greinert (1994), Kutscha (1995), and CEDEFOP (1995).

[18] For all paragraphs of the Vocational Training Act mentioned in the following, corresponding paragraphs can be found in the Crafts Code.

[19] For a list of other elements of the system indicating its duality, see Wilson (1997, p. 439). As in-company training is often supplemented by training at external training centres (Greinert, 1994, pp. 94–97) run by the Chambers or private providers, it has been argued that the term 'Dual' is too ambiguous to describe accurately the relationship between training in enterprises and vocational schools (Kutscha, 1996, p. 10ff.)

[20] It was argued that the Chambers, therefore, not only supervise the outcomes of training (final examinations) but also the quality of the qualifications process (resources, trainers' qualification) by monitoring adherence to legally binding regulations and standards. This is a marked difference to outcome-oriented modular systems, for instance NVQs in England (Reuling, 1997, p. 64ff.; Rützel, 1997, p. 6). For some of the problems the Chambers are facing in fulfilling these quality control functions, see Dougherty (1987, p. 172ff.), Raggatt (1988) and Deissinger (1996b).

As the quality control of VET provisions by a combination of regulative measures concerning both outcomes and input seems to be well accepted in the German context, it is one basis for the strategy of modularisation proposed in chapter 6.

[21] For the exact processes involved in developing recognised occupations, see Kutscha (1996, p. 22ff.) and Benner (1997a).

[22] The widespread consensus in Germany about the value of education and training, and strong commitment to it in practice, was moulded into the expression 'training culture' by British observers (Brown & Evans, 1994, p. 5).

[23] An agreement of the social partners and the federal government in 1995 aims to reduce the time for the updating process to 2 years (Benner, 1996, p. 3).

[24] Adaptation of a diagram of Münch (1991, p. 48).

[25] The author is aware of the semantic difficulties of the translation of the German term *Beruf*. As neither 'vocation' nor 'profession' is congruent to the German term, the former is chosen for this study because the latter appears to be too closely bound to academic occupations (e.g. lawyers, doctors, teachers).

[26] Kutscha regards the 'concept of the vocation', which represents also the basis of a vocational structured employment system, as the centrepiece of the Dual System (1995, p. 11), rather than the 'imaginary' duality of training places (1992, p. 539).

[27] This restrictive regulation implies the need for developing and continuously updating the training occupations in line with the vocationally oriented labour markets (*berufsfachliche Arbeitsmärkte*). For the theory of this type of labour market, see Sengenberger (1987, pp. 126–149).

As a consequence of this process, training occupations are well established amongst employers and employees. Clear evidence is provided by a study which shows that two-thirds of all job advertisements only state the training occupation to describe the job in question (Kloas, 1991, p. 25).

[28] The elements of occupational profiles are explained in more detail in chapter 6 as they play an important role in the proposed strategy of modularisation outlined in this chapter.

[29] As Kloas (1995, p. 3ff.) elaborates, an initial training qualification is obligatory for most forms of state-subsidised further training or retraining.

[30] For the most frequently stipulated requirements in connection with the concept of 'key qualifications', see Pätzold (1995) and Schelten & Glöggler (1992).

The primary ways to implement the concept within the didactic training practice may be regarded as project learning (Ertl, 1995, pp. 17–21, 48–56), cross-subject learning (Schelten, 1994), increased cooperation of vocational schools and training companies (Pätzold, 1997) and activity-oriented learning (Pätzold, 1992). The publications referenced here have to be regarded as an illustration of the intense debate in the specialist literature.

For a critical analysis of the use of the term 'key qualification' in the context of the functions of qualifications within society, cf. Beck (1980).

[31] Cf. Kloas (1997b, pp. 21–24). The categorisation is explicitly based on a German definition of vocation cf., for instance, a sociology-based definition by Beck et al (1980, p. 20) which contains most of the elements of the categorisation in a very condensed form. They defined vocation as: *combinations and delimitations of specialised, standardised and institutionalised labour models that are relatively independent of specific activities but also related to these activities. Amongst other things, these combinations are traded as commodities in exchange for payment in externally determined labour and production processes within a co-operative business structure.* (my translation)

[32] Interestingly, the literal German translation of 'initial qualifications' is not often used. Its equivalent, *Ausbildung*, is used congruently in most cases but the meaning of the English term 'a basis to further training' cannot be found in the German word.

[33] Some observers regard it as a model which has had its day and should be phased out; others regard it as a highly successful export commodity which will be the model for VET not only in the EU but also in the countries of the former Communist Bloc (cf. Arnold, 1993, p. 20ff.; Heimerer, 1995, p. 166). For the influence of the German system on educational policy and practice in other countries, see Wilson (1997, p. 437).

[34] Sloane (1997a, p. 233) speaks of a double-sided crisis within the system. On one hand, large training companies are reducing their training places because of the high costs, and on the other hand, small- and medium-sized firms have difficulties finding suitable trainees, as their training provisions do not appear attractive enough to gifted young people in contrast to higher education. Kloas (1994, p. 136ff.) questions the statistical bases of many studies concerned with the figures for supply and demand of training places.

For empirical studies on current and future training supply and demand see Parmentier et al (1994), Tessaring (1996), and for the relevant statistics in the last two years see BMBF (1997a, 1998).

[35] Cf. Müller & Schaarschuch (1996, p. 9) and Deissinger (1996b, p. 324). It has even been argued that the Dual System is not in crisis but its institutions are (Schmidt, 1996a, p. 2); in particular, the *Berufsschule* seems to have been in need of reform for over a decade now, as the didactic shortcomings and the 'identity crises' caused by improving in-company training in the larger training enterprises were already identified by Kloss (1985).

[36] For instance Kutscha (1993, 1997) advocates the development of the Dual System to a 'Plural System', which would not only integrate learning

venues like external training centres and polytechnics (*Fachhochschulen*) into the training structure but also school-based training courses outside the Dual System (cf. Rosenau, 1997, p. 11).

[37] All quotations and definitions referred to in this section can be found in appendix II.

[38] Nasta (1994, p. 81ff.) identifies starting a curriculum design process from the whole as the predominant practice in England, whereas starting from the module is widespread in the American system.

[39] My emphases.

[40] In Kloas's assumptions, the social standards are determined by the German 'concept of the vocation' (Kloas, 1997b, pp. 13, 17).

[41] Adaptation from Kloas's (1997b, p. 17) definition. The given characteristics are derived from an illustrative example in appendix III. Furthermore, the characteristics of modules in selected approaches of modularisation in selected European countries given in chapter 4 and appendix IV may serve as an illustration.

Theodossin (1986, pp. 9–16) identifies primary (seize, arrangement, assessment) and secondary (choice, sharing, 'tyranny of counting') characteristics of modules. Interestingly, there are substantial overlaps compared to the list given here despite the fact that Theodossin's definition is clearly set in an Anglo-American context and concentrates on the higher education sector.

[42] This attempt to conceptualise modularisation in VET is based on similar accounts by Deissinger (1996a, p. 192ff.), Zedler (1996, p. 20ff.), Sloane (1997a, pp. 227–231), Rützel (1997, p. 5ff.) and Kloas (1997b, p. 11ff.) For a conceptualisation of modular approaches in the United Kingdom covering not only VET, see Young (1995, p. 171ff.) Chapter 4 and appendix IV provide examples of how the ideal-typical concepts work in the practice of selected European countries.

[43] The training of assistants in craft professions is an example of the combination of initial and further training (cf. Braukmann & Sloane, 1994). This opportunity of combining different areas of training in a modularised system is a constant theme in the wider context of discussions in the EU, in which the demand for a more integrated training system runs like a thread through all relevant publications (Sellin, 1994a, p. 306).

[44] One example of an institutionally separated, additional qualification in initial training is the 'qualification of foreign language for trainees in commercial occupations' offered by some Chambers of Industry and Commerce (Zedler, 1996, p. 20).

[45] For example, this development was observed in pilot schemes preparing apprentices with university entrance qualifications for senior positions in small- and medium-sized craft firms (Sloane, 1992).

[46] Cf., for example, the drive for more modules for additional qualifications made by the Industry and Trade Advisory Board for Vocational Education (Zedler, 1996, p. 21).

[47] An example of this dismantling of existing vocational profiles is the modular approach in the Dutch printing industry as explained in chapter 4 and appendix IV.

[48] Commentators in Germany suggest the introduction of a so-called 'passport of vocational education' (*Berufsbildungspaß*) to record successfully completed modules (cf. Kloas 1997b, pp. 35, 47ff.) This passport could also facilitate the recognition of qualifications in the context of the free mobility of labour within the EU and is suggested by the European Council (Zimmermann, 1993, p. 340; Schmidt, 1996a, p. 25; Münk, 1995, p. 37). For the strategy of modularisation proposed in chapter 6, such a 'passport' assumes the function of the accrediting instrument for individual modules.

In a bilateral British–German seminar concerned with modularisation in VET, it was emphasised that both countries share an interest in a device to credit part-qualifications. The experiences with the Record of Achievement in Britain may provide valuable insights of advantages and dangers of a similar record in Germany. It was agreed to continue exchanging experiences in this matter (BMBF, 1997b, p. 36).

[49] Institutionally, the *Kollegschule* or 'College School' integrated vocational schools (*Berufsschule*) and schools leading to the general university entrance examination (*Gymnasium*). The curricula of these schools were combined with the means of a building brick system, which made vocational and academic qualifications open for modules from the other sphere of knowledge (cf. Blankertz, 1972a, 1972b; Office for Standards in Education [OFSTED], 1994a). For the 'concept of the vocation' in these schools, see Kell (1991).

[50] For some of the emerging issues of modular strategies for overcoming the academic/vocational division in Scotland, cf. Raffe (1994).

[51] Fauser et al (1983, p. 136) termed this process the '*Gymnasialisierung*' of the whole educational system.

[52] Commentators often discuss the challenges posed by these global economic and labour market trends under the rubric of post-Fordism. For the consequences of these trends in training and employment, see Gleeson (1995, p. 154ff.); Symes (1995, pp. 254–258); Fuller (1996, p. 230ff.) and Sharp (1996, p. 25ff.)

[53] For comprehensive accounts of these developments, see, for example, Barnard (1995) and Ertl (1998a).

[54] The Treaties set up the European Economic Community (EEC) and the European Atomic Energy Committee (EURATOM). In the relevant literature, the two Treaties are almost exclusively referred to as the 'Treaty of Rome'. This study will follow this convention.

[55] CEDEFOP developed the SEDOC (Register of Occupations and Professions in International Exchange) in cooperation with experts from all member states. The register contains descriptions of occupational profiles and the basic requirements of occupations for the allocation of diplomas, certificates and other evidence of qualifications recognised by the respective member states, and for comparison purposes (Sellin, 1996, p. 21ff.)

For details on the EC Programme *Comparability of Vocational Training Qualifications*, see Sellin (1992).

For the reasons for the limited success of the SEDOC Register in the member states and recent developments in the question of recognition and comparability, see Scheerer (1998) and Bjørnåvold & Sellin (1998).

[56] The Gravier case and the ERASMUS case may be the most influential rulings in a series of verdicts (cf. Hochbaum, 1989; Oppermann, 1991, p. 716ff.; Lane, 1993, p. 947ff.; Delgado & Losa, 1997, p. 133ff.)

[57] Strømnes notes that 28 EC programmes and projects in the field of education and training were executed in the 10 years after 1976 (Strømnes, 1997, p. 218). A variety of publications deal with European educational projects and programmes, i.e. Preston (1991), Funnell & Müller (1991, ch. 4), Kirby & Lamb (1997).

[58] For the full text of the two Articles see Phillips (1995a, p. 10ff.)

[59] Cf., for example, European Trade Union Committee for Education ([ETUCE] 1995), CEDEFOP (1995), Sellin (1996), Europäische Kommission (1996), Delgado & Losa (1997), Rubio (1997), Hörner (1997), Führ (1997).

[60] For a description of the functions and duration of the programmes, see Piehl & Sellin (1996).

[61] For a list of motives, expressed by employers in the Union, for the employment of mobile workers, see Scheerer (1998, p. 20).

[62] For accounts of these three strategies to fulfil the need for comparable qualifications in the EU, see, for example, CEDEFOP (1993), Zimmermann (1993), Feuchthofen (1993), Münk (1995, pp. 36–39), Sellin (1996), Müller-Solger (1997). For the latest developments in this question see the CEDEFOP publications, Bjørnåvold & Sellin (1998) and Scheerer (1998).

A new approach to create transparency between qualifications in different EU countries is described by Jens Schmidt (1997). In an Irish–German cooperation project, Irish electricians and motor mechanics sat the corresponding German initial training examinations. As they achieved similar or even slightly better results than their German counterparts, it might be concluded that the training standards of both countries in these fields are comparable.

[63] Conclusion of the European Council in Florence, June 1996; quoted in Münk (1997, p. 6). Münk goes on to identify further evidence for the

increasing convergence pressure on national systems. Cf. also Cleve & Kell (1996, p. 16ff.)

[64] Clear evidence for this reluctance can be identified in the analysis of the member states' statements concerning the aforementioned *Memorandum* of the Commission for Community policy. This analysis shows that all of the then 12 member states rejected the assumption of more legislative powers by the Commission. Notably, Denmark, Germany and the United Kingdom insisted strongly on the principle of subsidiarity in this question (Lipsmeier & Münk, 1994, pp. 132–175; Commission of the European Communities, 1994). Some commentators stress the danger that subsidiarity is not only used for the wholesale rejection of any forms of harmonisation, but also for blocking sensible processes of convergence by adapting best practice in other countries to improve their own national system of VET (Koch, 1996, p. 6).

[65] This potential is the main reason why modularity as a hypothesis is employed as an axiom in the philosophy of science to integrate areas of science which were regarded as incompatible hitherto. For such an attempt in theoretical linguistics, see Kertész (1991).

[66] Consequently, the information given in the table and in appendix IV is primarily drawn from articles about the EU project in question: Manning (1994, 1996), Sellin (1994b), Bruijn & Howieson (1995), Cleve & Kell (1996), Deissinger (1996a). For a short overview of modular strategies in VET in 12 countries of the EU, see Wiegand (1996a, pp. 264–268). Further references for the four individual countries are given in appendix IV.

[67] The details in this column are only valid for modularisation in the printing industry. For a more general overview of modular strategies in the Netherlands, see Bruijn & Howieson (1995).

[68] Cf. Noah & Eckstein (1988, p. 59ff.)

[69] The concepts are developed in chapter 3. Inevitably, this classification of the national approaches towards modularisation as described in the table and in appendix IV must be inaccurate to a certain extent, as the concepts developed in chapter 3 represent ideal-typical forms of modular structures.

[70] Cf. appendix V. For details about the development of the idea of a European dimension in education in the European movement before and after 1976 (including not only the European Community but also the Council of Europe and other institutions), see Haigh (1970), Neave (1984), Ryba (1992, 1995), Lagner (1997).

[71] Ryba (1992, p. 22ff.) compares official national views regarding the incorporation of the European dimension in education with the opinions of non-official but expert commentators in the countries concerned. His findings emphasise an enormous gulf between realities perceived by policy-makers and educational practitioners. He concludes that fundamentally different timescales and an emphasis on project-type activities instead of the creation of self-sustained programmes are the

main reasons for the relative failure of the implementation of the European dimension in education.

Lagner (1997, p. 29ff.) identifies the main obstacles for a more efficient introduction of the concept in German schools as the lack of cohesive strategies on a national level, subject-based methods of teaching and the lack of appropriate teaching materials. The latter obstacle is currently being tackled by the Council of Europe's *European Dimension Pedagogical Materials Programme* (*EDPM Programme*) (Ryba, 1997).

For a most recent account on the European dimension see Field (1998).

[72] For example, the PETRA programme provided 42 million ECU between 1992 and 1994 for 'developing European training modules for joint training of trainers' (Sellin, 1991, p. 9).

[73] For a more detailed and graphic explanation of this two-level cooperation model, cf. Sloane (1993, pp. 105–108).

[74] For the graph and its interpretation, cf. Sloane (1993, pp. 108–123 and 1997, p. 234ff.)

[75] The inner part of Sloane's model is closely related to the didactic approach developed by Paul Heimann, Wolfgang Schulz and Günter Otto in the 1960s and 1970s (*Lehr-/Lerntheoretische Didaktik der 'Berliner Schule'*). For a more detailed explanation of this approach, cf. Jank & Meyer (1994, pp. 181–233).

[76] The model could also be applied to a strategy of modularisation for the whole VET sector in Germany, cf. chapter 6.

[77] Noah & Eckstein (1998, pp. 45–52) argue that, in the 1970s and 1980s, the lack of adequate preparation of young people for the world of work was not only perceived by politicians and industry leaders in Britain but also in other countries, such as France and Germany.

[78] Already in the 1960s, the paradigm of state non-intervention was broken when the *Industrial Training Act* came into effect in 1964 (Page, 1967). This act has been regarded as the end of the *laissez-faire* period in the training sector in Britain, which started even before the Industrial Revolution (Deissinger & Greuling, 1994, p. 132; Deissinger, 1996b, p. 317).

[79] For a critical comparison of standards in education and training in Britain with those in Germany, cf. Prais (1981) and Prais & Wagner (1985).

[80] For the particular problems and the gradual decline of the British apprenticeship model, see Williams (1963), Deissinger (1994, pp. 27–30) and Unwin (1996, pp. 58–63). For the declining number of apprentices in the 1980s and 1990s, see Spours (1995a, p. 48).

[81] The different kinds of programmes under the YTS (employer-based, college-based) had the following aspects in common: opportunity to gain qualification by off-the-job training, including periods of work experience, opportunity to develop personal skills for all unemployed young people who did not remain in full-time education after the age of

16 (Pring, 1995, p. 54). Following the publication of the MSC Report *Development of the Youth Training Scheme* (also known as the Reay Report), youth training schemes were extended from 1 to 2 years (FEU, 1990, p. 12).

Despite its admirable intentions (creation of a national training system for school-leavers at the age of 16), YTS continues to be seen as a low-status option for low-skilled jobs, following the traditional low status of vocational education in Britain. The reason many employers have taken part in YTS has been financial incentives rather than commitment to high quality training. For critical accounts of YTS, see, for instance, Raffe (1990) and Martin (1993).

[82] The modular approach in education can be traced back to the development of *Programmed Instruction* by B. F. Skinner at Harvard University during the 1950s. In these instructions, small units of subject matter were used to teach students (Postlethwait, 1985, p. 3398). In English universities, modular courses first began to appear in the 1960s and grew in the 1970s (FEU, 1990, p. 30). In particular, the polytechnics, which gained university status in 1992, developed extensive modular structures (Stanyer, 1997, p. 37).

At around the same time, the International Labour Organisation (ILO), a United Nations Agency based in Geneva, started to develop a system of 'Modules of Employable Skills' (MES) to overcome the problems in VET in Third World countries. The main objective of MES is to reduce the costs of establishing a training sector in demographically rapidly growing societies with substantial deficits in basic education (Sellin, 1994b, p. 5). For the influence of MES on VET in industrial countries in general and in England in the 1970s, see Maslankowski (1985).

[83] Undeniably, large-scale modular developments in Scotland (cf. Raffe, 1994) had a major influence on the spread of the modular movement into VET in England and Wales (Jessup, 1991, p. 31).

[84] Cornford (1997, p. 238ff.) argues that modularisation and the competency-based approach have common roots in behavioural principles. Therefore, in the United Kingdom (but also in Australia), CBET and modularisation have come to be closely linked. The articles by Tuxworth (1989) and Young (1995) suggest that both the modular- and the competency-oriented approach were developing simultaneously during the educational reform period in the USA of the 1920s, and combined in US teacher training projects in the 1960s (cf. also Houston, 1985). Tuxworth (1989) describes how modularisation gained importance in the wake of the competency-based approach in the field of vocational education and training from the mid-1980s onwards.

[85] For the modular approach of the BTEC National Certificate, see Roberts (1987, pp. 235–239). BTEC merged with London University Examinations and Assessment Council to form EDEXCEL in 1996.

[86] Richardson et al (1995a, p. 9ff.) describe three stages of these developments in the school sector, which cannot be followed up in the present study.

[87] For the development of CAT and the approaches towards modularity, see the FEU publications: 1990, 1992, 1993 and 1995.

[88] For the debate on a unified post-16 curriculum, see Young et al (1994) and Young & Spours (1998).

[89] Richardson et al (1995a) visited over 30 institutions covering a range of different educational sectors and found a surprising diversity of modular approaches.

[90] This debate has produced an enormous amount of literature and even a very brief overview of the most important publications would go far beyond the scope of this study. The following studies are especially representative: Hyland (1994a); Burke (1989, 1995); Hodkinson & Issitt (1995); Pring (1995); Tomlinson (1997) and the literature mentioned in the last section of chapter 5.

[91] Table V summarises the temporal account of developments as set out in the following sources: Raggatt & Unwin (1991, pp. x–xv), Richardson (1995a, pp. 4–12), Richardson et al (1995b, p. 3ff.), Stanyer (1997, pp. 37–43), Young & Spours (1998, pp. 87–92).

For modular developments in Britain from the 1960s onwards, see Theodossin (1986, ch. 3) and Roberts (1987).

[92] On 1 October 1997, the Qualifications and Curriculum Authority (QCA) brought together the work of NCVQ and the School Curriculum and Assessment Authority (SCAA). An explicit aim of the new body was to end the academic/vocational divide in education (QCA, 1997a, p. 1).

[93] For a list of the shortcomings in VET as identified by the Review, see Jessup (1991, p. 10).

For more details on the implementation of NVQs, see, for instance, Field (1995, p. 32ff.); Stanton (1997, pp. 43–46).

[94] Raffe (1990, p. 58ff.) argued that these deficits were the result of two incongruent objectives of YTS: to react to the collapse of youth employment after 1979 on the one hand and to create a cohesive training structure on the other. The tension between these two functions resulted in inefficiency. For example, at the end of the 1980s, 27% of young people in Britain took part in YTS but only 29% of them attained a vocational certificate (Cleve & Kell, 1996, p. 17).

[95] All qualifications fall into a framework consisting of 11 *areas of competence:*

Tending animals, plants and land; Extracting and providing natural resources; Constructing; Engineering; Manufacturing; Transporting; Providing goods and services; Providing health, social and protective services; Providing business services; Communicating; Developing and extending knowledge and skill (QCA, 1997b, p. 5).

[96] This diagram represents an adaptation of illustrations in the following sources: Jessup (1991, p. 43), Ecclestone (1992), Nasta (1994, p. 17), Mansfield & Mitchell (1996, p. XXV), QCA (1997c, p. 10) and QCA (1997b, p. 2ff.)

[97] Information in this and the next section is drawn from *NVQ Criteria and Guidance* (NCVQ, 1995).

[98] Mansfield & Mitchell (1996) devote a chapter to each of these components (chs 9–11). The explanation here concentrates only on the major principles.

[99] Cf. Jessup (1991, p. 17).

[100] Jessup (1991, pp. 31–37) and Mansfield & Mitchell (1996) explain these structures in detail and give examples. One of these examples can be found in appendix VII.

[101] Adaptation of an illustration by Mathews, reprinted in Mansfield & Mitchell (1996, p. 201).

[102] Cf. the functions of the three types of units as described in chapter 5 on GNVQs.

[103] On average, nine units form a qualification (Richter, 1996, p. 39).

[104] The NCVQ has argued in this context that:
a sensible balance needs to be struck between, on the one hand, the breadth needed in setting national occupational targets for learners, and, on the other hand, achievability by candidates and relevance to employers. (NCVQ, 1995, p. 12)
It has been argued that the principles for the combination of units to NVQs are comparable to those which determine the formation of state-recognised training occupations in Germany (Stanyer, 1997, p. 56). Nevertheless, Deissinger (1996a, p. 198) challenges this assumption.

[105] The NRA was introduced in 1991 with the aim of establishing it as a universally recognised record of achievement spanning different forms of education and training. The NRA is currently under review due to its limited success (Kloas, 1997c, p. 36).

[106] For the origins, rationale and practice of task analysis and functional analysis, see Mansfield & Mitchell (1996, chs 5–8).
Sambrook & Steward (1995) identify eight steps of functional analysis instead of: 'the Employment Department's preferred method of producing statements of national standards' (p. 94). They question the philosophical and conceptual basis of functional analysis with the result that 'it seems safe ... to conclude that to locate functional analysis at the centre of reform of the UK system of vocational education is a questionable policy' (p. 104).

[107] For the criteria of assessment of NVQs and the problems involved, see Mansfield & Mitchell (1996, ch. 12–14).
Bierhoff & Prais (1997, p. 86ff.) suggest that assessment at the workplace is not considered objective in most European countries.

[108] In practice, there are time restrictions as units are only valid for certain periods of time, depending on their content. Furthermore, funding for training is often limited to a specific training period (Stanyer, 1997, p. 55).

[109] In this context, increased flexibility could be achieved by the new CREDIS system in Wales, which assigns a certain credit value to each unit. Used as an overall framework, this could lead the way to a more flexible use of units in different qualifications, not only in the training sector (Stanyer, 1997, pp. 50, 56).

[110] Stanton (1997, p. 48) describes this as an 'unrealistic schedule for implementation' which made it necessary to review and reform (Capey, 1995) the GNVQ provisions from as early as 1994 onwards.

[111] GNVQs can be seen in the tradition of pre-vocational courses (e.g. TVEI, CPVE in the 1980s), which emphasise personal preparation for an unpredictable future by the continuation of general education in a vocationally relevant form (Pring, 1993, pp. 104–113; 1995, p. 59ff.; 1997, pp. 30–36). This pre-vocational character seems to be incompatible with the demands of BTEC, employers' organisations and the Employment Department to make GNVQs more vocational and more job-related (Spours, 1995b, p. 14).

[112] The 15 *vocational areas* of GNVQs are: Health & Social Care; Leisure & Tourism; Business; Art & Design; Manufacturing; Science; Construction & the Built Environment; Hospitality & Catering; Engineering; Information Technology; Retail & Distributive Services; Media: Communication & Production; Management Studies; Land & Environmental Studies; Performing Arts & Entertainment Industries (QCA, 1997b, p. 52). The organisation of qualifications into vocational areas rather than subjects is a distinct difference to academic qualifications like GCSEs or A levels.

[113] This double objective of GNVQs has been regarded as their main problem. For instance, Smithers (1993) argues that as they try to prepare for both the world of work and higher education, GNVQs fail at both of the two objectives. They are characterised by a 'hybrid formation' which would inevitably result in pedagogic contradictions (Spours, 1995b, p. 19).

[114] The details given in the next sections are primarily drawn from City and Guilds (1993), BTEC (1994 and 1995) and NCVQ et al (1995). Further details can be found in the sources quoted in the sections.

[115] Further key differences between GNVQs and NVQs are identified in the subsequent sections and can be found in Hayward (1995, p. 15) and Spours (1995b, p. 15). For the debate as to whether GNVQs differ substantially from NVQs or not, see, for instance, Hyland (1994, p. 106ff.)

[116] It has been argued that delivery structures of GNVQs are regarded as a 'second order issue' with the result that there is an enormous variability of GNVQ standards (OFSTED, 1994b) and that the approaches towards the qualification vary greatly (Spours, 1995b, p. 17).

[117] For the roles and responsibilities in running GNVQ courses, see Hayward (1995, Table 1.5).

[118] Jessup (1995, p. 42) argues that this learning approach promotes the acquisition of cognitive skills for a vocational environment more than traditional, academic learning approaches.

[119] For details on assessment of GNVQs and changes of assessment arrangements in autumn 1995, see Capey (1995, appendix B) and Cotton & Robbins (1996, ch. 3).

[120] Adaptation of diagrams by Jessup (1991, p. 20; 1995, p. 36).

[121] As an example of the coverage in the mass media, the Channel 4 Report, *All Our Futures: Britain's education revolution* (Smithers, 1993), should be mentioned. For a summary of critiques in British newspapers, see Geb (1997).

[122] Deissinger (1996a, p. 201) describes this tendency of the NVQ framework as the 'balkanisation' of vocational qualifications. He argues that this is markedly different from recognised training occupations in Germany, where even the elements of occupational profiles are oriented towards comprehensive occupations valid for a whole vocational field (p. 197).

[123] Cornford (1997, p. 247) suggests the application of learning theories like Bruner's Spiral Curriculum in the design process of modules to overcome the danger caused by the behaviourist character of competency-based training.

[124] For the development of structuralist theory in linguistics and anthropology, see Levi-Strauss (1963) and Chomsky (1969).

[125] This strategy draws on proposals by Kloas (1997a, 1997b, 1997c) and Rützel (1997). A similar approach towards modularisation is currently being tested in four pilot projects for the part-time training of adults in work (Davids, 1996).

The strategy proposed here seeks to minimise the dangers of modularisation frequently stressed in German publications (cf. Cleve & Kell, 1996, p. 20; Manning, 1996, p. 309; Wiegand, 1996a, p. 268ff.; Rützel, 1997, p. 9).

[126] The positive effects of a 'qualification passport' (*Qualifizierungspaß*) have already been shown in a pilot project for the retraining of adults (Collingro & Dellbrück, 1997).

[127] For a comprehensive account of advantages, see Kloas (1997a, pp. 20–25).

[128] A pilot project by German Telecom has shown how additional and remedial modules can supplement recognised training occupations (Cleve, 1995, p. 13ff.)

[129] Käselau (1997) shows by the example of a number of companies in Berlin that modularity can substantially rationalise the cooperation of training companies with similar training needs.

[130] Cleve & Kell (1996, p. 20) argue that modularity in VET would inevitably result in fundamental debates about the role of the training sector within

the educational system and its functions in society. For the *Berufsschule*, this could lead to a severe identity crisis. Furthermore, a debate about modularity in the wider context of academic and vocational qualifications outside the provisions of the Dual System would be inevitable (Cleve & Kell, 1997, p. 4).

[131] The issue of whether didactic concepts derived from the ideas of 'key qualifications', like 'comprehensiveness', 'project method', and 'action-orientation', are really new or if they are just 'constantly reinventing the wheel' (Semel, 1992, p. 19) will not be considered in this study as it has already been discussed at some length (Ertl, 1995).

[132] Cf. Kutscha (1995, p. 14).

[133] The study 'The End of the Division of Labour?' (Kern & Schumann, 1984) should be mentioned here as probably the most influential in a series of research projects in the 1980s to investigate the scope and direction of changes in company organisation and rationalisation.

[134] In a follow-up study, Schumann et al (1994) admitted that the changes were not as far-reaching as predicted 10 years earlier.

[135] Cf. Kutscha (1995, p. 13ff.) For other examples that also include the off-the-job training in vocational schools, see the references given in the section on 'The "Concept of the Vocation"' in chapter 2.

[136] For sequencing mechanisms based on the theory of activity-oriented learning, see Ebner (1992).

[137] Definitions from German texts represent my translation. Emphases are mine.

[138] For the CEDEFOP system of qualification levels, see Gordon (1993, p. 91ff.)

[139] The information given here is primarily drawn from articles about the EU project introduced in chapter 4: Manning (1994, 1996), Sellin (1994b), Bruijn & Howieson (1995), Cleve & Kell (1996), Deissinger (1996a). Further references for the four individual countries are given in the following notes.

[140] For further details on VET in Spain after the 1990 reform act, see Collins (1993, ch. 12), Justicia (1995) and Padilla (1995).

[141] For further details on VET in France, see Department for Education (1993), Collins (1993, ch. 4), CEDEFOP (1994a) and Rothe (1995) (comparison of VET in Germany and France).

[142] This hierarchy ranges from level I (holder of a higher education postgraduate degree) to level VI (unskilled worker). Whereas a completed CAP qualification constitutes level V, CFI-modules as part of the *Unités Capitalisables* (UC), are classified at level V minus. For the complete hierarchy and the system of UCs, cf. Rothe (1995, pp. 104,108).

[143] The information on modularisation in the Dutch printing industry is drawn from Cleve (1994). For further details on VET in the Netherlands, see Collins (1993, ch. 10) and CEDEFOP (1994b).

[144] Reuling & Sauter (1996, p. 7) conclude that the whole Dutch system of vocational education and training will eventually become modularised.

[145] For diagrams of the system, see Cleve (1994, pp. 152–155).

[146] The modular concept of VET in Scotland is described in more detail in Further Education Staff College (1990), Raffe (1994) and Stanyer (1997); for the modular system in the context of assessment practices in Scottish education, see Brown (1991).

[147] The Scottish Education Department's *Action Plan* of 1983, which provided the basis for reorganising the whole non-academic post-16 sector in education, is regarded as a reaction to the threat of a takeover of the Scottish system by the central government in the shape of the Department of Employment's Manpower Services Commission (MSC) (Ainley, 1990, p. 113).

[148] For a more detailed discussion of potentials and dangers of the 'system focus' and the 'skill focus' of modularisation (e.g. the tension of creating a responsive *and* coherent system), see Bruijn & Howieson (1995).

[149] Cf. Resolution of the Council of Ministers of Education Meeting within the Council on the European Dimension in Education of 24 May 1988, 88/C177/02 (Council of Ministers, 1988).

[150] Cf. QCA (1997b, p. 5ff.)

[151] Adaptation of illustrations in Hayward (1995, pp. 16, 18) and descriptions by Collins (1993, p. 193ff.), Jessup (1995, p. 37ff.), BTEC (1995, p. 12ff.), Spours (1995b, p. 19ff.) and Stanyer (1997, p. 42ff.)

[152] Example taken from Jessup (1991, p. 37).

[153] Example adapted from BTEC (1994, Part I, p. 17).

References

Abel, Heinrich (1963) Von der Fortbildungsschule zur Berufsschule – die Lehrplandiskussion der neunziger Jahre, *Die Deutsche Berufs- und Fachschule*, 59, pp. 91–100.

Ainley, Patrick (1990) *Vocational Education and Training*. London: Cassell.

Arnold, Rolf (1993) Das duale System, *Berufsbildung in Wissenschaft und Praxis*, 22, pp. 20–27.

Aron, Raymond (1967) *Main Currents in Sociological Thought. Durkheim, Pareto, Weber*. New York: Basic Books.

Barnard, Catherine (1995) The Treaty on European Union, Education and Vocational Training, in David Phillips, *Aspects of Education and the European Union*, pp. 13–28. Oxford Studies in Comparative Education, vol. 5. Wallingford: Triangle.

Beaumont, Gordon (1995) *Review of 100 NVQs and SVQs. A Report Submitted to the Department for Education and Employment by Gordon Beaumont*. London: NCVQ.

Beck, Klaus (1980) Zum Problem des Verhältnisses von Mensch und Arbeit. Ein Vorschlag zur systematischen und terminologischen Präzisierung des Qualifikationsbegriffs am Beispiel der Berufswahl, *Zeitschrift für Berufs- und Wirtschaftspädagogik*, 76, pp. 355–364.

Beck, Ulrich, Brater, Hansjürgen & Daheim, Michael (1980) *Soziologie der Arbeit und der Berufe. Grundlagen Problemfelder, Forschungsergebnisse*. Reinbek: Rowohlt.

Beckers, Hans Joachim (1997) Modularakkreditierung und Personalzertifizierung. Deutsche Aus- und Weiterbildung unter europäischem Druck, *Wirtschafts- und Berufserziehung*, 6, pp. 217–224.

Bender, Thomas (1995) Leonardo da Vinci – Berufsbildung für Europa, in Kuratorium der Deutschen Wirtschaft (Ed.) *Berufliche Bildung in sich wandelndem betrieblichen Umfeld. Fachtagung 1995 der gewerblich-technischen Ausbilder*, pp. 18–24. Bonn: Kuratorium der Deutschen Wirtschaft.

Benner, Hermann (1992) Die duale Berufsausbildung in Deutschland und Aspekte ihrer Weiterentwicklung im Hinblick auf die europäische Integration, *Berufsbildung in Wissenschaft und Praxis*, 21, pp. 2–7.

Benner Hermann (1996) BIBB-Positionen zu aktuellen Herausforderungen in der beruflichen Bildung: I. Beruf und Berufskonzept, *Berufsbildung in Wissenschaft und Praxis*, 25, p. 3ff.

Benner, Hermann (1997a) Entwicklung anerkannter Ausbildungsberufe – Fortschreibung überkommener Regelungen oder Definition zukunftsbezogener Ausbildungsgänge? in Dieter Euler & Peter F. E. Sloane (Eds) *Duales System im Umbruch. Eine Bestandsaufnahme der Modernisierungsdebatte,* pp. 53–69. Pfaffenweiler: Centaurus-Verl.-Ges.

Benner, Hermann (1997b) Dreisprachige Ausbildungsprofile – neues Mittel zur Transparenz der Qualifikation anerkannter Ausbildungsberufe, *Berufsbildung in Wissenschaft und Praxis,* 26, p. 39ff.

Bierhoff, Helvia & Prais, Sigbert Jon (1997) *From School to Productive Work. Britain and Switzerland Compared.* Cambridge: Cambridge University Press.

Bjørnåvold, Jens & Sellin, Burkhart (1998) *Recognition and Transparency of Vocational Qualification; the way forward.* Thessaloniki: CEDEFOP.

Blankertz, Herwig (1972a) Kollegstufenversuch in Nordrhein-Westfalen – das Ende der gymnasialen Oberstufe und der Berufsschule, *Deutsche Berufs- und Fachschule,* 68, pp. 2–20.

Blankertz, Herwig (1972b) Rede anläßlich der Übergabe der Empfehlung zum Kollegstufenmodell Nordrhein-Westfalen an Herrn Kultusminister Girgensohn am 20.12.1971, *Deutsche Berufs- und Fachschule,* 68, pp. 565–568.

Braukmann, Ulrich & Sloane, Peter F.E. (1994) Flexibilisierung und Individualisierung der Ausbildung durch Zusatzqualifikationen, *Kölner Zeitschrift für Wirtschaft und Pädagogik,* 16, pp. 27–57.

Braun, Gaby (1994) NVQs and Modularisation: the approach taken by the Birmingham Metropolitan Institute of Technology, in John Twining (Ed.) *Competence & Assessment. Compendium No. 3. A Current Digest of the Latest Thinking and Best Practice,* pp. 26–31. London: Quarterly Journal of the Employment Department's Learning Methods Branch.

Brock, Colin & Tulasiewicz, Withold (Eds) (1994) *Education in a Single Europe.* London: Routledge.

Brown, Sally (1991) Assessment in the Scottish Education System, *Journal of Curriculum Studies,* 23, pp. 539–544.

Brown, Alan & Evans, Karen (1994) Changing the Training Culture: lessons from Anglo-German comparisons of vocational education and training, *British Journal of Education and Work,* 7, pp. 5–15.

Bruijn, E. de & Howieson, C. (1995) Modular Vocational Education and Training in Scotland and The Netherlands: between specificity and coherence, *Comparative Education,* 31, pp. 83–99.

Bundesministerium für Bildung, Wissenschaft, Forschung und Technologie (BMBF) (Ed.) (1997a) *Modularisierung der Berufsbildung – Gleichwertigkeit von allgemeiner und beruflicher Bildung. Deutsch-Britisches Seminar zur Berufsbildungspolitik 3–5 Februar 1997 in Berlin.* Bonn: BMBF.

Bundesministerium für Bildung, Wissenschaft, Forschung und Technologie (BMBF) (Ed.) (1997b) *Berufsbildungsbericht 1997.* Bonn: BMBF.

Bundesministerium für Bildung, Wissenschaft, Forschung und Technologie (BMBF) (Ed.) (1998) *Berufsbildungsbericht 1998.* Bonn: BMBF.

Burke, John W. (Ed.) (1989) *Competency Based Education and Training*. London: Falmer Press.

Burke, John (Ed.) (1995) *Outcomes, Learning and the Curriculum. Implications for NVQs, GNVQs and Other Qualifications*. London: Falmer Press.

Business and Technology Education Council (BTEC) (1994) *Getting GNVQs Right. Part I: Developing GNVQ Programmes; Part II: Teaching, Learning and Assessing; Part III: Building Portfolios; Part IV: Managing Quality*. London: BTEC.

Business and Technology Education Council (BTEC) (1995) *The GNVQ Question and Answer Guide*. London: BTEC.

Butterfield, Sue (1998) Conditions for Choice? The Context for Implementations of Curricular Pathways in the Curriculum, 14–16, in England and Wales, *Cambridge Journal of Education*, 28, pp. 9–20.

Callaghan, James (1976) Speech at Ruskin College, Oxford, in *The Times Educational Supplement*, 22 October 1976.

Callendar, Claire (1997) *Individual Take-up of NVQs/SVQs*. DfEE Research Studies RS 48. London: Department for Education and Employment.

Cantor, Leonhard (1989) *Vocational Education and Training in the Developed World*. London: Routledge.

Capey, John (1995) *GNVQ Assessment Review. Final Report of the Review Group Chaired by Dr John* Capey. London: NCVQ.

CEDEFOP (European Centre for the Development of Vocational Training) (1993) *Use of the System of Comparability of Vocational Training Qualifications by Employers and Workers. European Report*. Berlin: CEDEFOP.

CEDEFOP (European Centre for the Development of Vocational Training) (1994a) *Vocational Education and Training in France*. Berlin: CEDEFOP.

CEDEFOP (European Centre for the Development of Vocational Training) (1994b) *Vocational Education and Training in the Netherlands*. Berlin: CEDEFOP.

CEDEFOP (European Centre for the Development of Vocational Training) (1995) *Vocational Education and Training in the Federal Republic of Germany*. Berlin: CEDEFOP.

Chomsky, Noam (1969) *Aspects of the Theory of Syntax*. Cambridge: MIT Press.

City and Guilds (1993) *GNVQ Handbook*. London: City and Guilds of London Institute.

Cleve, Bernd van (1994) Zur Reform der Berufsausbildung innerhalb der Druckindustrie der Niederlande. Berufsbildung zwischen Modularisierung und Allgemeinbildung, *Zeitschrift für Berufs- und Wirtschaftspädagogik*, 90, pp. 147–158.

Cleve, Bernd van (1995) Module in der Aus- und Weiterbildung, *Gewerkschaftliche Bildungspolitik*, 1, pp. 12–18.

Cleve, Bernd van & Kell, Adolf (1996) Modularisierung der Berufsbildung, *Die berufsbildende Schule*, 48, pp. 15–22.

Cleve, Bernd van & Kell, Adolf (1997) Module in der beruflichen Bildung: Reformoption oder Deformationsvirus, *Berufsbildung*, 43, p. 4.

Coffey, David (1992) *Schools and Work. Developments in Vocational Education*. London: Cassell.

Collingro, Peter & Dellbrück, Joachim (1997) Modularisierte Nach-Qualifizierung von langzeitarbeitslosen jungen Erwachsenen, *Berufsbildung*, 43, pp. 19–21.

Collins, Helen (1993) *European Vocational Education Systems. A Guide to Vocational Education and Training in the European Community*. London: Kogan Page.

Commission of the European Communities (1990) *Proposal for a Council Decision Concerning an Action Programme for the Vocational Qualification of Young People and their Preparation for Adult and Working Life* (COM [90] 467 final of 9 November).

Commission of the European Communities (1991) *Memorandum of Vocational Training in the EC in the 1990s* (COM [91] 397 final of 12 December).

Commission of the European Communities (1993) *Green Paper on the European Dimension of Education*. Brussels and Luxembourg: Office for Official Publications of the European Communities.

Commission of the European Communities (1994) *Vocational Training in the European Community: challenges and future outlook: follow-up of the Commission Memorandum of Vocational Training in the EC in the* 1990s. Brussels and Luxembourg: Office for Official Publications of the European Communities.

Cornford, Ian R. (1997) Ensuring Effective Learning from Modular Courses: a cognitive psychology-skill learning perspective, *Journal of Vocational Education and Training*, 49, pp. 237–251.

Cotton, Julie & Robbins, Dennis (1996) *The Theory of GNVQ Planning & Assessment*. London: Kogan Page.

Council of Ministers (1988) *Resolution of the Council and the Ministers of Education Meeting within the Council on the European Dimension in Education of 24 May 1988*, 88/C177/02.

Davids, Sabine (1996) Berufsbegleitende Nachqualifizierung von Erwachsenen ohne Berufsausbildung – Realisierung eines modularen Konzepts in vier Modellversuchen, in Peter Diepold (Ed.) *Berufliche Aus- und Weiterbildung. Konvergenzen/Divergenzen, neue Anforderungen/alte Strukturen. Dokumentation des 2 Forums Berufsbildungsforschung 1995 an der Humboldt-Universität* zu Berlin, pp. 158–170. Beiträge zur Arbeitsmarkt- und Berufsforschung, BeitrAB 195. Nuremberg: Institut für Arbeitsmarkt- und Berufsforschung der Bundesanstalt für Arbeit.

Dearing, Sir Ron (1996) *Review of Qualifications for 16–19 Year Olds*. London: School Curriculum and Assessment Authority.

Deissinger, Thomas (1992) *Die englische Berufserziehung im Zeitalter der industriellen Revolution*. Würzburg: Königshausen und Neumann.

Deissinger, Thomas (1994) The Evolution of the Modern Vocational Training Systems in England and Germany: a comparative view, *Compare*, 24, pp. 17–36.

Deissinger, Thomas (1996a) Modularisierung der Berufsausbildung. – Eine didaktisch-curriculare Alternative zum Berufsprinzip? in Klaus Beck &

Frank Achtenhagen (Eds) *Berufserziehung im Umbruch. Didaktische Herausforderungen und Ansätze zu ihrer Bewältigung*, pp. 189–207. Weinheim: Beltz.

Deissinger, Thomas (1996b) Germany's Vocational Training Act: its functions as an instrument of quality control within a tradition-based vocational training system, *Oxford Review of Education*, 22, pp. 317–336.

Deissinger, Thomas & Greuling, Oliver (1994) Die englische Berufsbildungspolitik der achtziger Jahre im Zeichen der Krise eines Ausbildungssystems: Historische Hintergründe und aktuelle Problemlagen, *Zeitschrift für Berufs- und Wirtschaftspädagogik*, 90, pp. 127–146.

Delgado, I. Lirola Del & Losa, J. Jueyo (1997) Educational Policy in the European Union and the Principle of Subsidiarity: legal aspects and diverse areas of action, in Miguel Anxo Santos Rego (Ed.) *Política educativa en la Unión Europea despuétes de Maastricht* [Educational policy in the European Union after Maastricht], pp. 125–169. Santiago de Compostela: Colección Monografías.

Department for Education (DfE) (1993) *Aspects of Vocational Education in France*. London: HMSO.

Dougherty, Christopher (1987) The German Dual System: a heretical view, reprinted in David Phillips (Ed.) (1995) *Education in Germany. Tradition and Reform in Historical Context*, pp. 171–175. London and New York: Routledge.

Ebner, Hermann G. (1992) Facetten und Elemente didaktischer Handlungsorientierung, in Günter Pätzold (Ed.) *Handlungsorientierung in der beruflichen Bildung*, pp. 33–53. Frankfurt am Main: Gesellschaft zur Förderung Arbeitsorientierter Forschung und Bildung.

Ecclestone, Kathryn (1992) *Understanding Accreditation: ways of recognising achievement*. London: Unit for the Development of Adult Continuing Education.

Employment Department (ED) (1981) *A New Training Initiative: a consultative* document. London: HMSO.

Encyclopaedia Britannica (1997) CD-ROM Version 1.1.

Ertl, Hubert (1995) *Möglichkeiten und Grenzen der Umsetzung des reformpädagogischen Ideenguts von Helen Parkhurst an kaufmännischen Berufsschulen. Eine berufspädagogische Untersuchung*. Hamburg: Diplomarbeitsagentur.

Ertl, Hubert (1998a) The Provisions of the European Union in the Field of Vocational Education and Training, in *Münchner Texte zur Wirtschaftspädagogik*, vol. 6. Munich: Institut für Wirtschafts- und Sozialpädagogik an der Ludwig-Maximilians-Universität München.

Ertl, Hubert (1998b) Modern Apprenticeship Scheme – ein Neuanfang für die Lehre in England und Wales? *Kölner Zeitschrift für Wirtschaft und Pädagogik*, pp. 171–187.

Europäische Kommission (1996) *Weißbuch zur allgemeinen und beruflichen Bildung. Lehren und Lernen – Auf dem Weg zur kognitiven* Gesellschaft. Luxembourg: Amt für amtliche Veröffentlichungen der Europäischen Gemeinschaft.

European Commission (1996) White Paper on Education and Training: teaching and learning – towards a learning society. Luxembourg: Office for Official Publications of the European Communities.

European Trade Union Committee for Education (ETUCE) (1995) *Vocational Education in the European Union*. Brussels: ETUCE.

Fahle, Klaus (1995) Leonardo da Vinci – Berufsbildung für Europa, in Kuratorium der Deutschen Wirtschaft (Ed.) *Berufliche Bildung in sich wandelndem betrieblichen Umfeld. Fachtagung 1995 der gewerblich-technischen Ausbilde*, pp. 25–27. Bonn: Kuratorium der Deutschen Wirtschaft.

Fauser, Peter, Fintelmann, Klaus-J. & Flitner, Andreas (Eds) (1983) *Lernen mit Kopf und Hand. Bericht und Anstöße zum praktischen Lernen in der Schule.* Weinheim: Beltz.

Federal Minister for Education and Science (Ed.) (1992) *Vocational Training in the Dual System in the Federal Republic of Germany. An investment in the future.* Cologne: Kölnische Verlagsdruckerei.

Feuchthofen, Jörg (1993) Gleichwertigkeit beruflicher Bildungsabschlüsse in Europa, *Wirtschaft und Berufserziehung*, 45, pp. 73–79.

Field, John (1995) Reality Testing in the Workplace: are NVQs employer-led? in Phil Hodkinson & Mary Issitt (Eds) *The Challenge of Competence. Professionalism through Vocational Education and Training*, pp. 28–43. London: Cassell.

Field, John (1998) *European Dimensions. Education, Training and the European Union.* Higher Education Policy Series 39. London: Jessica Kingsley.

Finegold, David & Soskice, David (1988) The Failure of Training in Britain. Analysis and Prescription, *Oxford Review of Economic Policy*, 4, pp. 21–53.

Finegold, David, Keep, Ewart, Miliband, David, Raffe, David, Spours, Ken & Young, Michael (1990) *A British Baccalauréat. Ending the Division between Education and Training.* Education and Training Paper No. 1. London: Institute for Public Policy Research.

Flynn, James (1988) Vocational Training in Community Law and Practice, *Yearbook of European Law*, vol. 8, pp. 55–63.

Franklin, Kenneth (1997) National Vocational Qualifications, Scottish Vocational Qualifications and Competence-based Education and Training: from de Ville to Beaumont, *Journal of Vocational Education and Training*, 49, pp. 511–530.

Führ, Christoph (1997) *Deutsches Bildungswesen seit 1945. Grundzüge und Probleme.* Berlin: Luchterhand Verlag.

Fuller, Alison (1996) Modern Apprenticeship, Process and Learning: some emerging issues, *Journal of Vocational Education and Training*, 48, pp. 229–248.

Funnell, Peter & Müller, Dave (Eds) (1991) *Vocational Education and the Challenge of Europe. Responding to the Implications of the Single European Market.* New Developments in Vocational Education. London: Kogan Page.

Further Education Staff College (FESC) (1990)*The National Certificate in Scotland: five years on.* Combe Lodge Report, vol. 22, no. 4.

Further Education Unit (FEU) (1990) *Curriculum Development through YTS Modular Credit Accumulation*. London: FEU.

Further Education Unit (FEU) (1992) *A Basis for Credit? Developing a Post-16 Credit Accumulation and Transfer Framework. A Paper for Discussion.* London: FEU.

Further Education Unit (FEU) (1993) *A Basis for Credit? Developing a Post-16 Credit Accumulation and Transfer Framework. Feedback and Discussion.* London: FEU.

Further Education Unit (FEU) (1995) *A Framework for Credit. A Common Framework for Post-14 Education and Training for the Twenty-first Century.* London: FEU.

Geb, Natalie (1997) Das britische Modulsystem der beruflichen Bildung im Spiegel der eigenen Presse, *Berufsbildung in Wissenschaft und Praxis*, 26, pp. 35–40.

Geissler, Karlheinz (1994) Von der Meisterschaft zur Qualifikations-Collage. Drei Entwicklungen, die industrielle Berufsausbildung gefährden, in Sabine Liesering, Karen Schober & Manfred Tessaring (Eds) *Die Zukunft der dualen Berufsausbildung. Eine Fachtagung der Bundesanstalt für Arbeit*, pp. 328–334. Beiträge zur Arbeitsmarkt- und Berufsforschung, BeitrAB 186. Nuremberg: Institut für Arbeitsmarkt- und Berufsforschung der Bundesanstalt für Arbeit.

Geissler, Karlheinz & Orthey, Frank Michael (1998) Am Ende des Berufs, *Süddeutsche Zeitung*, 17, p. 53.

Georg, Walter (1997) Berufliche Bildung zwischen Internationalisierung und nationaler Identität, in Christoph Kodron, Botho von Kopp, Uwe Lauterbach, Ulrich Schäfer & Gerlind Schmidt (Eds) *Vergleichende Erziehungswissenschaft: Herausforderung, Vermittlung, Praxis. Festschrift für Wolfgang Mitter zum 70 Geburtstag*, pp. 312–329. Köln: Böhlau Verlag.

Gleeson, Paul (1995) Restructuring the Industrial Trades in Australia: the dark side of post-Fordism, *Journal of Vocational Education and Training*, 47, pp. 153–164.

Gonon, Philipp (1998) Modularisierung als reflexive Modernisierung, in Dieter Euler (Ed.) *Berufliches Lernen im Wandel – Konsequenzen für die Lernorte? Dokumentation des 3 Forums Berufsbildungsforschung 1997 an der Friedrich-Alexander-Universität Erlangen-Nürnberg*, pp. 305–321. Beiträge zur Arbeitsmarkt- und Berufsforschung, BeitrAB 214. Nuremberg: Institut für Arbeitsmarkt- und Berufsforschung der Bundesanstalt für Arbeit.

Gordon, Jean (1993) *Systeme und Verfahren der Zertifizierung von Qualifikationen in der Europäischen Gemeinschaft*. Thessaloniki: CEDEFOP.

Greinert, Wolf-Dietrich (1994) *The 'German System' of Vocational Education. History, Organization, Prospects.* Studien zur Vergleichenden Berufspädagogik. Baden-Baden: Deutsche Gesellschaft für Technische Zusammenarbeit.

Groothoff, Hans-Hermann (Ed.) (1964) *Das Fischer Lexikon Pädagogik.* Neuausgabe. Frankfurt am Main: Fischer.

Haack, Claudio, Müller, Karlheinz & Weisschuh, Bernd (1996) Benötigen wir eine Modularisierung der Ausbildung? *Berufsbildung in Wissenschaft und Praxis*, 25, pp. 9–11.

Hagedorn, Jobst R. (1997) Modulare Ausbildung als Qualifizierungsweg für (gegenwärtig) nicht ausbildbare junge Menschen, *Gewerkschaftliche Bildungspolitik*, 11/12–97, pp. 16–18.

Hahn, Angela (1997) Vollzeitschulen und duales System – Alte Konkurrenzdebatte oder gemeinsame Antworten auf dringende Fragen? in Dieter Euler & Peter F. E. Sloane (Eds) *Duales System im Umbruch. Eine Bestandsaufnahme der Modernisierungsdebatte*, pp. 27–51. Pfaffenweiler: Centaurus-Verl.-Ges.

Haigh, Anthony (1970) *A Ministry of Education for Europe*. London: Harrap.

Hayward, Geoff (1995) *Getting to Grips with GNVQs. A Handbook for Teachers*. London: Kogan Page.

Heimerer, Leonhard (1995) Die Berufsschulen – sind besser als ihr Ruf, *Die berufsbildende Schule. Zeitschrift des Bundesverbandes der Lehrer an beruflichen Schulen*, 47, pp. 166–170.

Her Majesty s Inspectorate (HMI) (1991) *Aspects of Vocational Education and Training in the Federal Republic of Germany*. London: HSMO.

Her Majesty s Inspectorate (HMI) (1995) *Post-16 Vocational Education and Training in Germany. International Report*. London: Further Education Funding Council.

Heursen, Gerd (1983) Kompetenz – Performanz, in Dieter Lenzen & Klaus Mollenhauer (Eds) *Enzyklopädie Erziehungswissenschaft, Bd. 1: Theorie und Grundbegriffe der Erziehung und Bildung*, pp. 472–478. Stuttgart: Klett-Cotta.

Herz, Gerhard & Jäger, Angelika (1998) Module in der Berufsbildung oder des Kaisers neue Kleider? *Berufsbildung in Wissenschaft und Praxis*, 27, pp. 14–20.

Hochbaum, Ingo (1989) Das ERASMUS-Urteil des Europäischen Gerichtshofs, *Mitteilungen des deutschen Hochschulverbandes*, 4, pp. 156–189.

Hodkinson, Phil & Issitt, Mary (Eds) (1995) *The Challenge of Competence. Professionalism through Vocational Education and Training*. London: Cassell.

Hörner, Wolfgang (1997) Europa als Herausforderung für die Vergleichende Erziehungswissenschaft – Reflexionen über die politische Funktion einer pädagogischen Disziplin, in Christoph Kodron, Botho von Kopp, Uwe Lauterbach, Ulrich Schäfer & Gerlind Schmidt (Eds) *Vergleichende Erziehungswissenschaft: Herausforderung, Vermittlung, Praxis. Festschrift für Wolfgang Mitter zum 70 Geburtstag*, pp. 65–80. Köln: Böhlau Verlag.

Houston, W.R. (1985) Competency-based Teacher Education, in Torsten Husen & Neville T. Postlethwaite (Eds) *The International Encyclopaedia of Education*, pp. 898–906. Oxford: Pergamon Press.

Hyland, Terry (1994a) *Competence, Education and NVQs. Dissenting Perspectives*. London: Cassell.

Hyland, Terry (1994b) Silk Purses and Sows' Ears: NVQs, GNVQs and experiential learning, *Cambridge Journal of Education*, 24, pp. 233–243.

Hyland, Terry (1996) National Vocational Qualifications, Skills Training and Employers' Needs: beyond Beaumont and Dearing, *Journal of Vocational Education and Training*, 48, pp. 349–365.

Jank, Werner & Meyer, Hilbert (1994) *Didaktische Modelle*. Frankfurt am Main: Cornelsen Scriptor.

Jessup, Gilbert (1985) *Technical Note on the New Training Initiative: implications for standards, assessment procedures and accreditation*, reprinted in Gilbert Jessup (1991) *Outcomes. NVQs and the Emerging Model of Education and Training*, pp. 165–173. London: Falmer Press.

Jessup, Gilbert (1991) *Outcomes. NVQs and the Emerging Model of Education and Training*. London: Falmer Press.

Jessup, Gilbert (1995) Outcome Based Qualifications and Implications for Learning, in John Burke (Ed.) *Outcomes, Learning and the Curriculum. Implications for NVQ s, GNVQ s and Other Qualifications*, pp. 33–54. London: Falmer Press.

Joint Council of National Vocational Awarding Bodies (1995) Changes to Arrangements for Assessment of GNVQs for September 1995, reprinted as Appendix E in John Capey *GNVQ Assessment Review. Final Report of the Review Group Chaired by Dr John* Capey. London: NCVQ.

Justicia, Diego (1995) Vocational education in LOGSE: a new model for the future? in Oliver Boyd-Barrett & Pamela O'Malley (Eds) *Education Reform in Democratic Spain*, pp. 226–234. International Developments in School Reform. London: Routledge.

Käselau, Michael (1997) Module im Ausbildungsverbund – ein Lernkonzept zum Thema Trennen und Umformen, *Berufsbildung*, 43, pp. 27–29.

Kell, Adolf (1991) Berufsbezug in der Kollegschule. Theoretische Begründungen und konzeptionelle Konsequenzen, *Die berufsbildende Schule*, 43, pp. 296–319.

Kern, Horst & Schumann, Michael (1984) *Das Ende der Arbeitsteilung? Rationalisierung in der industriellen Produktion: Bestandsaufnahme, Trendbestimmung*. Munich: Beck.

Kertész, András (1991) *Die Modularität der Wissenschaft: konzeptuelle und soziale Prinzipien linguistischer Erkenntnis*. Brunswick: Vieweg.

Keune, Saskia & Zielke, Dietmar (1992) Individualisierung und Binnendifferenzierung: eine Perspektive für das duale System? *Berufsbildung in Wissenschaft und Praxis*, 21, pp. 32–37.

Kirby, Simon & Lamb, Muriel (1997) *Travelling, Studying, Working and Living within the European Union. Factsheet*. London: Representation of the European Commission in the United Kingdom.

Kloas, Peter-Werner (1991) *Was von Berufsanfängern verlangt wird – Anforderungsprofile in Stellenanzeigen*. Berichte zur beruflichen Bildung, Heft 118. Berlin: BIBB.

Kloas, Peter-Werner (1994) 10 Thesen zur Modernisierungs- und Differenzierungs-fähigkeit des dualen Berufsausbildungssystems, in Sabine

Liesering, Karen Schober & Manfred Tessaring (Eds) *Die Zukunft der dualen Berufsausbildung. Eine Fachtagung der Bundesanstalt für Arbeit*, pp. 136–142. Beiträge zur Arbeitsmarkt- und Berufsforschung, BeitrAB 186. Nuremberg: Institut für Arbeitsmarkt- und Berufsforschung der Bundesanstalt für Arbeit.

Kloas, Peter-Werner (1995) Qualifizierung in Beschäftigung – neue Ansätze zur beruflichen Integration von Problemgruppen des Arbeitsmarktes, *Berufsbildung in Wissenschaft und Praxis*, 24, pp. 3–10.

Kloas, Peter-Werner (1996) Modulare Weiterbildung im Verbund mit Beschäftigung – Arbeitsmarkt- und bildungspolitische Aspekte eines strittigen Ansatzes, *Berufsbildung in Wissenschaft und Praxis*, 25, pp. 39–46.

Kloas, Peter-Werner (1997a) *Modularisierung in der beruflichen Bildung. Modebegriff, Streitthema oder konstruktiver Ansatz zur Lösung von Zukunftsproblemen*. Berlin und Bonn: Bundesinstitut für Berufsbildung.

Kloas, Peter-Werner (1997b) Modulare Berufsausbildung in Deutschland: Streitthema ohne Wirkung oder Perspektive mit Zukunft? *Gewerkschaftliche Bildungspolitik*, 11/12–97, pp. 18–25.

Kloas, Peter-Werner (1997c) Berufskonzept und Modularisierung in der deutschen Berufsbildung, in Bundesministerium für Bildung, Wissenschaft, Forschung und Technologie (BMBF) (Ed.) *Modularisierung der Berufsbildung – Gleichwertigkeit von allgemeiner und beruflicher Bildung. Deutsch-Britisches Seminar zur Berufsbildungspolitik 3–5 Februar 1997 in Berlin*, pp. 15–36. Bonn: BMBF.

Kloss, Günther (1985) Vocational Education: a success story? in Günther Kloss (Ed.) *Education Policy in the Federal Republic of Germany 1969–1984*, pp. 100–114. Manchester: Department of Language and Linguistics, University of Manchester Institute of Science & Technology; reprinted in David Phillips (Ed.) *Education in Germany. Tradition and Reform in Historical Context*, pp. 161–170 London and New York: Routledge.

Koch, Richard (1994) Grundstrukturen der Mitwirkung der Sozialpartner in den Mitgliedsstaaten und auf der Gemeinschaftsebene, *Berufsbildung in Wissenschaft und Praxis*, 23, pp. 26–31.

Koch, Richard (1996) BIBB-Positionen zu aktuellen Herausforderungen in der beruflichen Bildung: IV. Verhältnis von EU-Politik und nationaler Berufsbildungspolitik, *Berufsbildung in Wissenschaft und Praxis*, 25, p. 6ff.

Kuda, Eva (1996) Steigerung der Attraktivität dualer Ausbildung durch praxisorientierte Kurzlehrgänge? *Berufsbildung in Wissenschaft und Praxis*, 25, pp. 16–20.

Kunkel, Wolfgang & Paluch, Iris (1997) Modularisierung und Qualitätssicherung in der Aus- und Weiterbildung, *Berufsbildung*, 43, pp. 13–15.

Kutscha, Günter (1992) Entberuflichung und Neue Beruflichkeit – Thesen und Aspekte zur Modernisierung der Berufsausbildung und ihrer Theorie, *Zeitschrift für Berufs- und Wirtschaftspädagogik*, 88, pp. 535–548.

Kutscha, Günter (1993) Modernisierung der Berufsausbildung im Spannungsfeld von Systemdifferenzierung und Koordination, in Friedrich Buttler, Reinhard Czycholl & Helmut Pütz (Eds) *Modernisierung beruflicher Bildung vor den Ansprüchen von Vereinheitlichung und Differenzierung*, pp. 40–62. Beiträge zur Arbeitsmarkt- und Berufsforschung, BeitrAB 177. Nuremberg: Institut für Arbeitsmarkt- und Berufsforschung der Bundesanstalt für Arbeit.

Kutscha, Günter (1995) General and Vocational Education and Training in Germany – continuity amid change and the need for radical modernization <http://www.uni-duisburg.de/FB2/BERU/download/vocation.zip> (55KB).

Kutscha, Günter (1996) Berufsbildungssystem und Berufsbildungspolitik, <http://www.uni-duisburg.de/FB2/BERU/download/berufpol.zip> (183KB).

Kutscha, Günter (1997) Integriertes Lernen in berufs- und studienbezogenen Bildungsgängen der Sekundarstufe II. Entwicklungen und Konzepte, in der Bundesrepublik Deutschland <http://www. uni-duisburg.de/FB2/BERU/download/integrat.zip> (24KB).

Kutscha, Günter (1998) Ausbildungsordnungen unter dem Einfluß der Internationalisierung und Pluralisierung von Industrienormen, in Dieter Euler (Ed.) *Berufliches Lernen im Wandel – Konsequenzen für die Lernorte? Dokumentation des 3 Forums Berufsbildungsforschung 1997 an der Friedrich-Alexander-Universität Erlangen-Nürnberg*, pp. 265–284. Beiträge zur Arbeitsmarkt- und Berufsforschung, BeitrAB 214. Nuremberg: Institut für Arbeitsmarkt- und Berufsforschung der Bundesanstalt für Arbeit.

Lagner, Uta B. (1997) Die europäische Dimension im beruflichen Bildungswesen – dargestellt am Modellversuch EUWAS, *Kölner Zeitschrift für Wirtschaft und Pädagogik*, 12, pp. 19–36.

Lane, Robert (1993) New Community Competences under the Maastricht Treaty, *Common Market Law Review*, 30, pp. 939–979.

Lauglo, Jon & Lillis, Kevin M. (Eds) (1988) *Vocationalizing Education*, Comparative and International Education Series, vol. 6. Oxford: Pergamon Press.

Levi-Strauss, Claude (1963) *Structural Anthropology*. New York: Basic Books.

Lipsmeier, Antonius (1978) *Organisation und Lernorte der Berufsausbildung*. Munich: Juventa Verlag.

Lipsmeier, Antonius & Münk, Dieter (1994) *Die Berufsbildungspolitik der Gemeinschaft für die 90er Jahre. Analyse der Stellungnahmen der EU-Mitgliedstaaten zum Memorandum der Kommission*. Bonn: Bundesministerium für Bildung und Wissenschaft.

Manning, Sabine (1994) Aspekte modularer Berufsausbildung – Ergebnisse von Interviews in sechs Ländern der Europäischen Union, *Berufsbildung in Wissenschaft und Praxis*, 23, p. 40ff.

Manning, Sabine (1996) Modularisierte Berufsausbildung als Chance für benachteiligte Jugendliche. Erkenntnisse aus einem europäischen Forschungsprojekt, *Die berufsbildende Schule*, 48, pp. 308–310.

Manpower Services Commission (MSC) (1981) *A New Training Initiative*. Sheffield: MSC.

Manpower Services Commission (MSC) (1984) *Standards in Clerical and Administrative Occupations: managing agents' guide to standard tasks*, partly reprinted in Gilbert Jessup (1991) *Outcomes. NVQs and the Emerging Model of Education and Training*, p. 32. London: Falmer Press.

Mansfield, Bob & Mitchell, Lindsay (1996) *Towards a Competent Workforce.* Aldershot: Gower.

Martin, Lindsay (1993) Training Credits, in Harry Tomlinson (Ed.) *Education & Training 14–19. Continuity and Diversity in the Curriculum*, pp. 164–181. London: Longman.

Maslankowski, Willi (1985) Berufsbildung in Teilqualifikationen. Der modulare Ansatz MES der Internationalen Arbeitsorganisation, *Zeitschrift für Berufs- und Wirtschaftspädagogik*, 81, pp. 323–331.

Mertens, Dieter (1974) Schlüsselqualifikationen. Thesen und Schulung für eine moderne Gesellschaft, *Mitteilungen aus der Arbeitsmarkt- und Berufsforschung*, 7, pp. 36–43.

Müller, Karlheinz & Schaarschuch, Andreas (1996) Das Entwicklungspotential des dualen Systems, *Berufsbildung in Wissenschaft und Praxis*, 25, pp. 9–12.

Müller-Solger, Hermann (1997) Anerkennung, Akkreditierung, Transparenz – Notwendige Begriffsklärungen für die Europäische Union, in Christoph Kodron, Botho von Kopp, Uwe Lauterbach, Ulrich Schäfer & Gerlind Schmidt (Eds) *Vergleichende Erziehungswissenschaft: Herausforderung, Vermittlung, Praxis. Festschrift für Wolfgang Mitter zum 70 Geburtstag*, pp. 245–261.. Köln: Böhlau Verlag.

Münch, Joachim (1991) *Vocational Training in the Federal Republic of Germany*, 3rd edn. Berlin: CEDEFOP.

Münk, Dieter (1995) Kein Grund zur Eu(ro)phorie. Anmerkungen zu zentralen berufsbildungspolitischen Kontroversen des Memorandums der Kommission über die Berufsausbildungspolitik der Gemeinschaft für die 90er Jahre, *Zeitschrift für Berufs- und Wirtschaftspädagogik*, 91, pp. 28–45.

Münk, Dieter (1997) Berufsausbildung in der EU zwischen Dualität und Monalität – eine Alternative ohne Alternative? *Berufsbildung*, 45, pp. 5–8.

Nasta, Tony (1994) *How to Design a Vocational Curriculum. A Practical Guide for Schools and Colleges.* London: Kogan Page.

National Council for Vocational Qualifications (NCVQ) (1989) *NVQ Criteria and Procedures.* London: NCVQ.

National Council for Vocational Qualifications (NCVQ) (1995) *NVQ Criteria and Guidance.* London: NCVQ.

National Council for Vocational Qualifications (NCVQ), BTEC, City and Guilds & RSA Examination Board (1995) *GNVQ Quality Framework. Quality Indicators and Guidance of Designing and Running GNVQ Courses.* London: NCVQ.

Neave, Guy (1984) *The EEC and Education.* Stoke-on-Trent: Trentham Books.

Neugebauer, Wolfgang (Ed.) (1992) *Schule und Absolutismus in Preussen. Akten zu preußischen Elementarschulwesen bis 1806.* Veröffentlichungen der Historischen Kommission zu Berlin, vol. 83. Berlin: Walter de Gruyter.

Noah, Harold J. (1984) The Use and Abuse of Comparative Education, *Comparative Education Review*, 28, pp. 550–562.

Noah, Harold J. & Eckstein, Max A. (1988) Business and Industry Involvement with Education in Britain, France and Germany, in Jon Lauglo & Kevin

M. Lillis (Eds) *Vocationalizing Education*, pp. 45–68, Comparative and International Education Series, vol. 6. Oxford: Pergamon Press.

Offe, Claus (1975) *Berufsbildungsreform. Eine Studie über Reformpolitik.* Frankfurt am Main: Suhrkamp.

Office for Standards in Education (OFSTED) (1994a) *The Development of Double Qualification Courses in Schools in North Rhine Westphalia. A Report From the Office of Her Majesty's Chief Inspector of Schools.* London: HMSO.

Office for Standards in Education (OFSTED) (1994b) *GNVQs in Schools 1993/94. Quality and Standards of General National Vocational Qualifications. A Report from the Office of Her Majesty's Chief Inspector of* Schools. London: HMSO.

Oppermann, Thomas (1991) *Europarecht: Eine Studie.* Juristische Kurzlehrbücher. Munich: Beck.

Orthey, Frank Michael (1998) Zwischen Ordnung und Unordnung – Berufsbildung im Modernisierungsprozeß, in Dieter Euler (Ed.) *Berufliches Lernen im Wandel – Konsequenzen für die Lernorte? Dokumentation des 3 Forums Berufsbildungsforschung 1997 an der Friedrich-Alexander-Universität Erlangen-Nürnberg*, pp. 285–304. Beiträge zur Arbeitsmarkt- und Berufsforschung, BeitrAB 214. Nuremberg: Institut für Arbeitsmarkt- und Berufsforschung der Bundesanstalt für Arbeit.

Otter, Sue (1996) Modularisation and Qualification Reform in the UK: some realities, in CEDEFOP *Pedagogic Innovation.* Vocational Training, European Journal, no. 7. Thessaloniki: CEDEFOP.

Padilla, Antonio José Gil (1995) Training and Employment, in Oliver Boyd-Barrett & Pamela O'Malley (Eds) *Education Reform in Democratic Spain*, pp. 235–245. International Developments in School Reform. London: Routledge.

Page, G. Terry (1967) *The Industrial Training Act and After.* London: Andre Deutsch.

Panorama DDR (foreign press agency of the former GDR) (1985) *Vocational Training: equal opportunities for all. The Options Open to Young People in the GDR.* Berlin: Zeit im Bild.

Parmentier, Klaus, Schober, Karen & Tessaring, Manfred (1994) Zur Lage der dualen Berufsausbildung in Deutschland. Neue empirische Ergebnisse aus dem IAB, in Sabine Liesering, Karen Schober & Manfred Tessaring (Eds) *Die Zukunft der dualen Berufsausbildung. Eine Fachtagung der Bundesanstalt für Arbeit*, pp. 7–47. Beiträge zur Arbeitsmarkt- und Berufsforschung, BeitrAB 186. Nuremberg: Institut für Arbeitsmarkt- und Berufsforschung der Bundesanstalt für Arbeit.

Pätzold, Günter (Ed.) (1992) *Handlungsorientierung in der beruflichen Bildung.* Frankfurt am Main: Gesellschaft zur Förderung Arbeitsorientierter Forschung und Bildung.

Pätzold, Günter (1995) Handlungsorientiertes Lehren und Lernen in der schulischen Berufsbildung. Notwendigkeit und Perspektiven aus Sicht der Berufs- und Wirtschaftspädagogik, *Die kaufmännische Schule*, 40, pp. 155–165.

Pätzold, Günter (1997) Lernortkooperation – wie ließe sich die Zusammenhanglosigkeit der Lernorte überwinden, in Dieter Euler & Peter F. E. Sloane (Eds) *Duales System im Umbruch. Eine Bestandsaufnahme der Modernisierungsdebatte*, pp. 121–142. Pfaffenweiler: Centaurus-Verl.-Ges.

Phillips, David (1994) Periodisation in Historical Approaches to Comparative Education: some considerations from the examples of Germany and England and Wales, *British Journal of Educational Studies*, 42, pp. 261–272.

Phillips, David (Ed.) (1995a) *Aspects of Education and the European Union*. Oxford Studies in Comparative Education, vol. 5. Wallingford: Triangle.

Phillips, David (Ed.) (1995b) *Education in Germany. Tradition and Reform in Historical Context*. London and New York: Routledge.

Piehl, Ernst & Sellin, Burkhart (1996) *Initial and Continuing Vocational Training in Europe*. First reprint. Thessaloniki: CEDEFOP.

Postlethwait, S.N. (1985) Module Approach, in Torsten Husen & Neville T. Postlethwaite (Eds) *The International Encyclopaedia of Education*, pp. 3398–3400. Oxford: Pergamon Press.

Prais, Sigbert Jon (1981) Vocational Qualifications of the Labour Force in Britain and Germany, *National Institute Economic Review*, 98, pp. 47–59.

Prais, Sigbert Jon (1989) How Europe Would See the New British Initiative for Standardising Vocational Qualifications, *National Institute Economic Review*, August, pp. 52–54.

Prais, Sigbert Jon & Wagner, Karin (1985) Schooling Standards in England and Germany: some summary comparisons bearing on economic performance, *National Institute Economic Review*, 112, S.53–76.

Preston, Jill (1991) *EC Education, Training and Research Programmes. An Action Guide*. London: Kogan Page.

Pring, Richard (1993) A Philosophical Perspective on 14–19 Curriculum Change, in Harry Tomlinson (Ed.) *Education & Training 14–19. Continuity and Diversity in the Curriculum*, pp. 96–113. London: Longman.

Pring, Richard (1995) *Closing the Gap: liberal education and vocational preparation*. London: Hodder & Stoughton.

Pring, Richard (1997) Aims, Values and the Curriculum, in Sally Tomlinson (Ed.) *Education 14–19. Critical Perspectives*, pp. 21–36. London: Athlone Press.

Pütz, Helmut (1997) Modularisierung – das falsche Thema, ungenügend bearbeitet, zur ungeeigneten Zeit, in Peter-Werner Kloas *Modularisierung in der beruflichen Bildung. Modebegriff, Streitthema oder konstruktiver Ansatz zur Lösung von Zukunftsproblemen*, pp. 62–75. Berlin und Bonn: Bundesinstitut für Berufsbildung.

Qualifications and Curriculum Authority (QCA) (1997a) *An Introduction*. London: QCA.

Qualifications and Curriculum Authority (QCA) (1997b) *Data News*. Issue 5, Autumn 1997. London: QCA.

Qualifications and Curriculum Authority (QCA) (1997c) *The Monitor*. Issue 5, Autumn 1997. London: QCA.

Raffe, David (1990) The Context of the Youth Training Scheme: an analysis of its strategy and development, in Denis Gleeson (Ed.) *Training and its Alternatives*, pp. 58–75. Milton Keynes: Open University Press.

Raffe, David (1994) Modular Strategies for Overcoming Academic/Vocational Divisions: issues arising from the Scottish experience, *Journal of Educational Policy*, 9, pp. 141–154.

Raggatt, Peter (1988) Quality Control in the Dual System of West Germany, reprinted in David Phillips (Ed.) (1995) *Education in Germany. Tradition and Reform in Historical Context*, pp. 176–202. London: Routledge.

Raggatt, Peter & Unwin, Lorna (Eds) (1991) *Change and Intervention. Vocational Education and Training*. London: Falmer Press.

Reuling, Jochen (1996) Modularisierung in der englischen Berufsbildung, *Berufsbildung in Wissenschaft und Praxis*, 25, pp. 48–52.

Reuling, Jochen (1997) Qualitätssicherung in der deutschen Berufsbildung durch kombinierte Verwendung von Input- und Outputkriterien, in Bundesministerium für Bildung, Wissenschaft, Forschung und Technologie (BMBF) (Ed.) (1997) *Modularisierung der Berufsbildung – Gleichwertigkeit von allgemeiner und beruflicher Bildung*, pp. 64–68. *Deutsch-Britisches Seminar zur Berufsbildungspolitik 3–5 Februar 1997 in Berlin*. Bonn: BMBF.

Reuling, Jochen & Sauter, Edgar (1996) BIBB-Positionen zu aktuellen Herausforderungen in der beruflichen Bildung: V. Modularisierung in der beruflichen Bildung, *Berufsbildung in Wissenschaft und Praxis*, 25, p. 6ff.

Richardson, William (1998) Work-based Learning for Young People: national policy, 1994–1997, *Journal of Vocational Education and Training*, 50, pp. 225–245.

Richardson, William, Spours, Ken, Woolhouse, John & Young, Michael (1995a) *Learning for the Future: current developments in modularity and credit*. Working Paper 5. London and Warwick, Institute of Education, Post-16 Education Centre, University of London & Centre for Education and Industry, University of Warwick.

Richardson, William, Spours, Ken, Woolhouse, John & Young, Michael (1995b) *Learning for the Future: current 14–19 education and training*. Working Paper 1. London and Warwick, Institute of Education, Post-16 Education Centre, University of London & Centre for Education and Industry, University of Warwick.

Richter, Ansgar (1996) Qualitativer und quantitativer Vergleich von Berufsbildungs-abschlüssen in Großbritannien und Deutschland, *Berufsbildung in Wissenschaft und Praxis*, 25, pp. 35–42.

Roberts, Iolo (1987) Modular Structures: their strengths and weaknesses, in John Twinning, Stanley Nisbet, & Jacquetta Megarry (Eds) (1987) *World Yearbook of Education 1987. Vocational Education*, pp. 233–246. London: Kogan Page.

Rosenau, Renate (1997) Berufsausbildung in Schulen, *Berufsbildung*, 45, pp. 9–11.

Rothe, Georg (1995) *Die Systeme beruflicher Qualifizierung Frankreichs und Deutschlands im Vergleich. Übereinstimmung und Besonderheiten in den Beziehungen zwischen den Bildungs- und Beschäftigungssystemen zweier Kernländer der EU*. Beiträge zur Arbeitsmarkt- und Berufsforschung, BeitrAB

190. Nuremberg: Institut für Arbeitsmarkt- und Berufsforschung der Bundesanstalt für Arbeit.

Rubio, Rogelio Medina (1997) The Setting of Competence for Education and Culture in the European Union Treaty, in Miguel Anxo Santos Rego (Ed.) *Política educativa en la Unión Europea despuétes de Maastricht* [Educational policy in the European Union after Maastricht], pp. 71–91. Santiago de Compostela: Colección Monografías.

Rudden, Bernard & Wyatt, Derrick (Eds) (1994) *Basic Community* Law, 5th edn. Oxford: Clarendon Press.

Rützel, Josef (1997) Reform der beruflichen Bildung durch Modularisierung, *Berufsbildung*, 43, pp. 5–9.

Ryba, Raymond (1992) Toward a European Dimension in Education. Intention and Reality in European Community Policy and Practice, *Comparative Education Review*, 36, pp. 10–24.

Ryba, Raymond (1995) Is Progress towards Development of the European Dimension in Education Satisfactory? in David Phillips (Ed.) *Aspects of Education and the European Union*, pp. 63–76. Oxford Studies in Comparative Education, vol. 5. Wallingford: Triangle.

Ryba, Raymond (1997) Developing the European Dimension of Education in Practice: The Contribution of the Council of Europe's European Dimension Pedagogical Materials Programme, in Christoph Kodron, Botho von Kopp, Uwe Lauterbach, Ulrich Schäfer & Gerlind Schmidt (Eds) *Vergleichende Erziehungswissenschaft: Herausforderung, Vermittlung, Praxis. Festschrift für Wolfgang Mitter zum 70 Geburtstag*, pp. 262–271. Köln: Böhlau Verlag.

Sadler, Michael (1900) How Far Can We Learn Anything of Practical Value from the Study of Foreign Systems of Education, in James Henry Higginson (1979) *Selections from Michael Sadler*. Liverpool: Dejall & Meyorre.

Sambrook, Sally & Steward, Jim (1995) The Role of Functional Analysis in National Vocational Qualifications: a critical appraisal, *British Journal of Education and Work*, 8, pp. 93–106.

Scheerer, Friedrich (1998) *Transparenz beruflicher Befähigungsnachweise in Europa. Stand und Entwicklungsperspektiven*. Thessaloniki: CEDEFOP.

Schelten, Andreas & Glöggler, Karl (1992) *Fächerübergreifender Unterricht in der Berufsschule: Konzept und Erkenntnisse im Schuljahr 1990/91: Bericht des Lehrstuhls für Pädagogik der Technischen Universität München über die wissenschaftliche Begleitung des Schulversuchs Fächerübergreifender Unterricht in der Berufsschule in Bayern*. Munich: Staatsinstitut für Schulpädagogik und Bildungsforschung.

Schelten, Andreas (1994) *Fächerübergreifender Unterricht in der Berufsschule. Ergänzung zur Verlaufsuntersuchung einer Konzeption in Altötting 1992: Nachtragsbericht des Lehrstuhls für Pädagogik der Technischen Universität München über die wissenschaftliche Begleitung des Schulversuchs Fächerübergreifender Unterricht in der Berufsschule in Bayern*. Munich: Technische Universität.

Schenk, Barbara (1992) Kollegschule, in Dieter Lenzen (Ed.) *Enzyklopädie Erziehungswissenschaft. Band 9: Sekundarstufe II – Jugendbildung zwischen*

Schule und Beruf, Teil 2: Lexikon (Eds: Herwig Blankertz, Josef Derbolav, Adolf Kell & Günter Kutscha), pp. 378–381. Stuttgart: Klett-Cotta.

Schmidt, Hermann (1996a) Das Prinzip der Partnerschaft in einem offenen europäischen Raum für Berufsausbildung und Qualifizierung, *Berufsbildung in Wissenschaft und Praxis*, 23, pp. 24–26.

Schmidt, Hermann (1996b) Flexibilisierung der Berufsausbildung – Flexibilisierung als Organisationsprinzip? *Berufsbildung in Wissenschaft und Praxis*, 25, p. 1ff.

Schmidt, Hermann (1997a) Vorwort, in Peter-Werner Kloas *Modularisierung in der beruflichen Bildung. Modebegriff, Streitthema oder konstruktiver Ansatz zur Lösung von Zukunftsproblemen*, p. 3ff. Berlin und Bonn: Bundesinstitut für Berufsbildung.

Schmidt, Hermann (1997b) Module in der Berufsbildung – Teufelszeug oder Ausweg aus der Krise? *Berufsbildung*, 43, p. 42.

Schmidt, Jens U. (1997) Empirischer Vergleich von irischen und deutschen Ausbildungsstandards, *Berufsbildung in Wissenschaft und Praxis*, 26, pp. 28–34.

Schumann, Michael (1994) Rationalisierung und Übergang – Neue Befunde der Industriesoziologie zum Wandel der Produktionskonzepte und Arbeitsstrukturen, *WSI Mitteilungen*, 47, pp. 405–414.

Sellin, Burkhart (1991) *Euroqualifications for All. New EC Approaches and Programmes for the Vocational Training of Young People*. Berlin: CEDEFOP.

Sellin, Burkhart (1992) *The EC Programme Comparability of Vocational Training Qualifications. Aims, Working Methods, Evaluation*. Berlin: CEDEFOP.

Sellin, Burkhart (1994a) Die Finanzierung der außerschulischen Berufsbildung in Europa, in Sabine Liesering, Karen Schober & Manfred Tessaring (Eds) *Die Zukunft der dualen Berufsausbildung. Eine Fachtagung der Bundesanstalt für Arbeit*, pp. 306–309. Beiträge zur Arbeitsmarkt- und Berufsforschung, BeitrAB 186. Nuremberg: Institut für Arbeitsmarkt- und Berufsforschung der Bundesanstalt für Arbeit.

Sellin, Burkhart (1994b) *Vocational Training in Europe: towards a modular form?* Thessaloniki: CEDEFOP.

Sellin, Burkhart (1996) *Do Joint European Vocational Training Standards Stand a Chance? Recognition and Transparency of Qualifications. Discussion Paper*. Thessaloniki: CEDEFOP.

Semel, Susan F. (1992) *The Dalton School. The Transformation of a Progressive School*. New York: Lang.

Sengenberger, Werner (1987) *Struktur und Funktionsweise von Arbeitsmärkten. Die Bundesrepublik im internationalen Vergleich*. Frankfurt am Main: Campus.

Sharp, Graham (1996) Post-Fordism, the Vocational Curriculum and the Challenge to Teacher Preparation, *Journal of Vocational Education and Training*, 48, pp. 25–39.

Simons, Diane (1966) *Georg Kerschensteiner. His Thought and Its Relevance Today*. London: Methuen.

Sloane, Peter F.E. (1992) *Modellversuchsforschung. Überlegungen zu einem wirtschaftspädagogischen Forschungsansatz.* Wirtschafts-, Berufs- und Sozialpädagogische Texte, vol. 18. Cologne: Müller Botermann.

Sloane, Peter F.E. (Ed.) (1993) *Transnationale Ausbildung im Handwerk.* Cologne: Carl.

Sloane, Peter F.E. (1997a) Modularisierung in der beruflichen Ausbildung – oder: Die Suche nach dem Ganzen, in Dieter Euler & Peter F. E. Sloane (Eds) *Duales System im Umbruch. Eine Bestandsaufnahme der Modernisierungsdebatte*, pp. 223–245. Pfaffenweiler: Centaurus-Verl.-Ges.

Sloane, Peter F.E. (1997b) Alte Theorie – neue Praxis – neue Theorie? Innenansichten von Berufsschullehrern und Ausbildern, in Adolf Kell & Jan-Hendrik Olbertz (Eds) *Vom Wünschbaren zum Machbaren. Erziehungswissenschaft in den neuen Bundesländern*, pp. 351–372. Weinheim: Beltz.

Smithers, Alan (1993) *All Our Futures: Britain's education revolution. Dispatches* Report on Education for Channel 4 Television.

Smithers, Alan (1995) Able to Dribble, but Not to Score? *Times Educational Supplement 2*, 10 February, p. 11.

Smithers, Alan (1997) A Critique of NVQs and GNVQs, in Sally Tomlinson (Ed.) *Education 14–19. Critical Perspectives*, pp. 55–70. London: Athlone Press.

Sparkes, John (1994) Wider Knowledge and Understanding, *Times Educational Supplement*, 16 December, p. 12.

Spilsbury, M., Moralee, J. & Evans, C. (1995) *Employers' Use of the NVQ System.* Institute of Employment Studies (IES) Report 293. Brighton: IES.

Spours, Ken (1995a) *Learning for the Future: strength and weaknesses of GNVQs: principles of design current developments in modularity and credit.* Working Paper 3. London and Warwick, Institute of Education, Post-16 Education Centre, University of London & Centre for Education and Industry, University of Warwick.

Spours, Ken (1995b) *Learning for the Future: post-compulsory education and training: statistical trends.* Working Paper 7. London and Warwick, Institute of Education, Post-16 Education Centre, University of London & Centre for Education and Industry, University of Warwick.

Spranger, Eduard (1920) Allgemeinbildung und Berufsschule, *Deutsche Fach- und Fortbildungsschule*, 14, pp. 313–324.

Stanton, Geoff (1997) Pattern in Development, in Sally Tomlinson (Ed.) *Education 14–19. Critical Perspectives*, pp. 37–54. London: Athlone Press.

Stanyer, Joe (1997) Die Kursstrukturen im Britischen Berufsbildungssystem, in Bundesministerium für Bildung, Wissenschaft, Forschung und Technologie (BMBF) (Ed.) *Modularisierung der Berufsbildung – Gleichwertigkeit von allgemeiner und beruflicher Bildung. Deutsch-Britisches Seminar zur Berufsbildungspolitik 3–5 Februar 1997 in Berlin*, pp. 37–60. Bonn: BMBF.

Strømnes, Åsmund L. (1997) Education as a Merger between Unity and Diversity, in Miguel Anxo Santos Rego (Ed.) *Política educativa en la Unión Europea despuétes de Maastricht* [Educational policy in the European Union after Maastricht], pp. 215–224. Santiago de Compostela: Colección Monografías.

Syfried, Brigitte (1997) Die Abschlußprüfung in der Berufsausbildung – ein Bremsklotz für Innovation?, in Dieter Euler & Peter F. E. Sloane (Eds) *Duales System im Umbruch. Eine Bestandsaufnahme der Modernisierungsdebatte*, pp. 345–360. Pfaffenweiler: Centaurus-Verl.-Ges.

Symes, Colin (1995) A Post-Fordist Reworking of Australian Education: the Finn, Mayer and Carmichael reports in the context of labour reprocessing, *Journal of Vocational Education and Training*, 47, pp. 247–271.

Taylor, Angus (1993) TVEI and the curriculum 14–18, in Harry Tomlinson (Ed.) *Education & Training 14–19. Continuity and Diversity in the Curriculum*, pp. 183–196. London: Longman.

Taylor, M.E. (1981) *Education and Work in the Federal Republic of Germany*. London: Anglo-German Foundation for the Study of Industrial Society.

Tessaring, Manfred (1996) Qualifikationsentwicklung bis 2010. Welche Trends bestimmen die langfristige Entwicklung unter besonderer Berücksichtigung von Aus- und Weiterbildung? in Peter Diepold (Ed.) *Berufliche Aus- und Weiterbildung. Konvergenzen/Divergenzen, neue Anforderungen/alte Strukturen. Dokumentation des 2 Forums Berufsbildungsforschung 1995 an der Humboldt-Universität zu* Berlin, pp. 277–288. Beiträge zur Arbeitsmarkt- und Berufsforschung, BeitrAB 195. Nuremberg: Institut für Arbeitsmarkt- und Berufsforschung der Bundesanstalt für Arbeit.

Theodossin, Ernest (1986) *The Modular Market. Studies in Further Education*. Bristol: Further Education Staff College.

Thyssen, Simon (1954) *Die Berufsschule in Idee und Gestaltung*. Essen: Girardet.

Tomlinson, Sally (Ed.) (1997) *Education 14–19. Critical Perspectives*. London: Athlone Press.

Tuxworth, Eric (1989) Competence Based Education and Training: background and origins, in John W. Burke (Ed.) (1989) *Competency Based Education and Training*, pp. 10–25. London: Falmer Press.

Unwin, Lorna (1996) Employer-led Realities: apprenticeship past and present, *Journal of Vocational Education and Training*, 48, pp. 57–68.

Wagner, Peter (1991) Science of Society Lost: on the failure to establish sociology in Europe during the Classical Period, in Peter Wagner, Björn Wittrock & Richard Whitley (Eds) *Discourses on Society. The Shaping of the Social Science Disciplines*, pp. 219–245. Dordrecht: Kluwer Academic Publishers.

Weinhuber, Karl (1997) Ein Modulsystem für die handwerkliche Ausbildung im Berufsfeld Farbtechnik und Raumgestaltung, *Berufsbildung*, 43, p. 25ff.

Wiegand, Ulrich (1996a) Reform des Ordnungsrahmens: Modulsysteme oder Flexibilisierung der Ausbildungsordnungen? in Winfried Schlaffke & Reinhold Weiß (Eds) *Das duale System der Berufsausbildung: Leistung, Qualität und Reformbedarf*, pp. 260–276. Kölner Texte & Thesen. Cologne: Hundt Druck.

Wiegand, Ulrich (1996b) Modules in vocational training, in CEDEFOP *Pedagogic Innovation*, pp. 28–30. Vocational Training, European Journal, no. 7. Thessaloniki: CEDEFOP.

Williams, G. (1963) *The Lesson for Britain*. London: Chapman & Hall.

Wilson, David N. (1997) The German Dual System of Vocational Education and Training: a comparative study of influence upon educational policy in other countries, in Christoph Kodron, Botho von Kopp, Uwe Lauterbach, Ulrich Schäfer & Gerlind Schmidt (Eds) *Vergleichende Erziehungswissenschaft: Herausforderung, Vermittlung, Praxis. Festschrift für Wolfgang Mitter zum 70 Geburtstag*, pp. 437–447. Köln: Böhlau Verlag.

Young, Michael, Hayton, Annette, Hodgson, Ann & Morris, Andrew (1994) An Interim Approach to Unifying the Post-16 Curriculum, in Sally Tomlinson (Ed.) *Educational Reform and its Consequences*, pp. 73–92. London: Rivers Oram Press.

Young, Michael (1995) Modularization and the Outcomes Approach: towards a strategy for a curriculum of the future, in John Burke (Ed.) *Outcomes, Learning and the Curriculum. Implications for NVQ s, GNVQ s and Other Qualifications*, pp. 169–181. London: Falmer Press.

Young, Michael & Spours, Ken (1998) 14–19 Education: legacy, opportunities and challenges, *Oxford Review of Education*, 24, pp. 83–97.

Zedler, Reinhard (1996) Some Remarks on Modular Training in the Federal Republic of Germany, in CEDEFOP *Pedagogic Innovation*, p. 20ff. Vocational Training, European Journal, no. 7. Thessaloniki: CEDEFOP.

Zedler, Reinhard (1997) Modularisierung: keine Perspektive für die Berufsausbildung, *Berufsbildung*, 43, p. 42.

Zentralverband des Deutschen Handwerks (ZDH) (1993) Beurteilung einer Ausbildung in Modulen aus der Sicht des ZDH, in Peter F.E. Sloane (Ed.) *Transnationale Ausbildung im Handwerk*, pp. 127–130. Cologne: Carl.

Zimmermann, Claudia (1993) Die Anerkennung von Berufsabschlüssen in Europa. Keine Klarheit bei der Berücksichtigung sozialer Berufe, *Soziale Sicherheit. Zeitschrift für Arbeitsmarkt- und Sozialpolitik*, 42, pp. 337–340.

APPENDICES

APPENDIX I. Micro-didactic Innovations of In-company Training in Germany

As described in chapter 2, the concept of 'key qualifications' and 'generic skills' started to influence training in the Dual System from the 1970s onwards. This appendix aims to show the consequences of these 'new' [131] ideas on in-company training at a micro-didactic level.

In order to understand the scope of change the new methods brought to the training process, one has to be aware of the traditional method of teaching that developed from the beginnings of the apprenticeship system in the craft trades which arose in the Middle Ages. The apprentice adopted the work techniques and skills of his master. He tried to imitate his master as closely as possible and to improve his skills by practising. In the 1920s and 1930s, this basic model was moulded into a linear sequence of steps when large industrial companies introduced means of standardised training for a large number of apprentices in order to create employees skilled for mass production. This process can be seen as the didactic integration of the Taylorist plant regime of labour division into the traditional German 'concept of the vocation' (chapter 2). The result of this integration process at a micro-didactic level was the 'Four-Step-Method', which dominated company-based training in Germany for the greater part of this century [132] (see Figure A1).

It is important to note that the Four-Step-Method was developed and used in strongly hierarchical and directional company structures. Its effectiveness was dependent on the clearly defined roles of the trainer (who has specialist knowledge and skills and who knows the only possible way of using them) and the trainee (who is willing to accept the dominant role of the trainer and to put aside his or her own interests and aspirations) in the learning process.

With the introduction of new, flexible production processes, primarily because of the rapid progress of information technology, the Taylorist division of work has started to lose its dominance.[133] Although the identification of a Taylorist and a post-Taylorist era is too simplistic and in spite of doubts as to the extent to which the new era of production processes has materialised [134], decentralisation, work in partly autonomous groups, and company-wide quality control measures have influenced training methods. New concepts have been developed to take the changed work environment into account. It was concluded that tasks and functions were no longer separate issues and this resulted in the skilled worker having to fulfil the formerly separated functions of planning, executing and controlling work tasks. Consequently, more complex and integrated training processes have had to be developed to enable the trainee to fulfil the new role. The traditional Four-Step-Method could not provide such processes.

Active Person	Stages of Activity
Trainer	1. Preparation
	2. Demonstration
Trainee	3. Imitation
	4. Exercise

Figure A1. The Four-Step-Method of company-based training.

The following outline represents one example of such new methods of in-company training, developed in the field of metalwork occupations but analogous to approaches in other fields.[135] The process in organised into six sequences [136] in which trainees solve complex work tasks.

- The trainees are given the tasks and basic explanations. For this sequence 'guiding texts' (prepared written materials that support independent learning) and interactive training programmes may be used.
- The trainees try to find the information they need on their own. They plan necessary steps and resources.
- The resulting plan is discussed with trainers, who also support decision-making.
- The trainees execute the plan unaided, in most cases in teamwork.
- The trainees control and assess the final product by themselves to learn to judge the quality of the work.
- After this process of self-monitoring, the trainees present their work to the trainers. Together they discuss problems and find conclusions to be drawn for future tasks.

This model is explicitly based on the trainees' actions, and thinking in comprehensive patterns and teamwork are fostered. This implies distinctly different roles for trainees and trainers to those in the Four-Step-Method. Kutscha (1995, p. 15) illustrated the concept as shown in Figure A2.

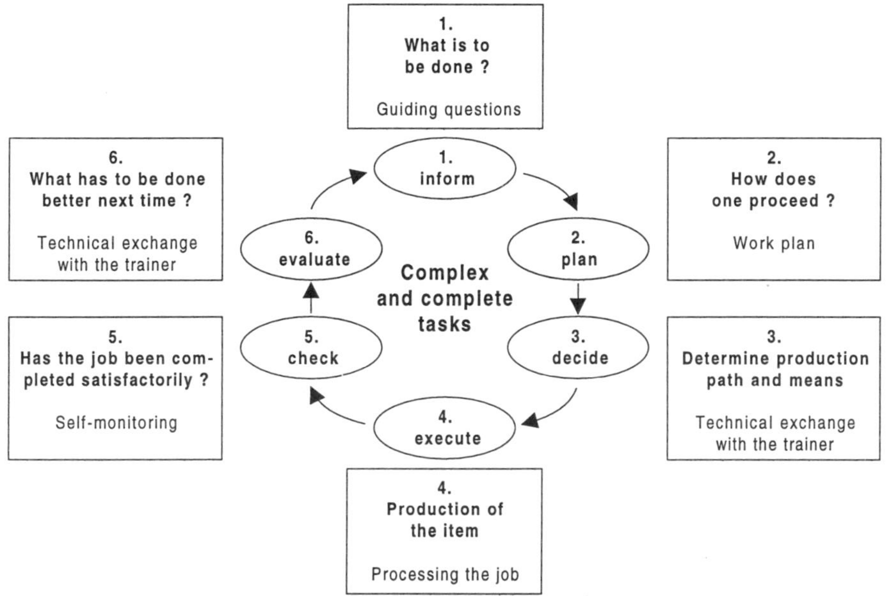

Figure A2. New concept for firm-based training: action-oriented learning.

APPENDIX II. Selected Module Definitions [137]

Ainley (1990, p. 84):

> Modules *are not a sequential division of the curriculum ... but a series of free-standing learning objectives with 'built up' effect: in other words, a module can stand alone or form part of a route picked through the various units on offer.*

Braun (1994, p. 26):

> Modularisation *is seen ... as the division of the curriculum into manageable parts for the purpose of delivery, in order primarily to improve access and progression.*
>
> Braun describes 11 types of modules, developed by the Birmingham Metropolitan Institute of Technology in their project to modularise the curriculum both for NVQs and other training provisions (Braun, 1994, p. 28ff.)

Cornford (1997, p. 238):

> Modularisation *of courses involves the packaging of course content, either theory or practical, into shorter, logically self-contained units which together cover the content which would be covered by a conventional, longer course.*

Deissinger (1996a, p. 191ff.):

> *In general, the term* 'module' *is used for standardised learning opportunities which refer to the acquisition of specific (vocational) competences and which – as a curricular element (including descriptions of the aims and/or the content of learning) – take on an institutionalised form. The basic feature of independence and differentiation from other curricular elements is decisive.*
> [Als 'Module' werden im allgemeinen standardisierte Lernangebote bezeichnet, die auf den Erwerb spezifischer (beruflicher) Kompetenzen verweisen und als curriculare Bausteine (mit Lernziel- und/oder Lerninhaltsbeschreibungen) eine institutionalisierte Form annehmen. Entscheidend ist das Grundmerkmal ihrer Eigenständigkeit und Abgegrenztheit gegenüber anderen curricularen Bausteinen.]

FEU (Further Education Unit) (1995, p. 6):

> *1. It is possible and helpful to define all awards, whether labelled 'academic' or 'vocational', in terms of the required* learning outcomes.
> *2. A unit is a coherent set of learning outcomes.*
> *3. It is important to distinguish between a* unit *of learning outcomes and a* module *of delivery, which is a sub set of a learning programme (such as a course of lectures, a work experience placement, or a project). For simplicity, one module is often designed to deliver one unit, but too rigid relationship between modules and units can inhibit flexibility and responsiveness.*

Jessup (1985, p. 171):

> *A* module *may be defined as a group of related skills and knowledge which forms a recognizable block of activity within an occupation or a subject.*

Kloas (1997b, p. 10ff.):

> *Up to the present day, there is no clear, comprehensive and universally binding definition of what is meant by modules in vocational education and training. If there is an agreement at all, it is valid only for a negative definition: Modules should be*

seen as separate from courses which are specified from start to end and which comprise longer lasting learning processes. The concept implies ideas of flexibility and shorter sequences of learning.
[Es gibt bisher keine eindeutige, umfassende und allgemeinverbindliche Definition dessen, was unter Modulen in der beruflichen Bildung zu verstehen sei. Wenn sich überhaupt Übereinstimmung festmachen läßt, so gilt sie nur für die Negativdefinition: Module sollen sich von Bildungsgängen abgrenzen, die vom Anfang bis zum Ende festgelegt sind und länger andauernde Lernprozesse umfassen. Vorstellungen von Flexibilität und kürzeren Lernsequenzen stehen dahinter.]

Nasta (1994, p. 81):

> *A* module *is a measurable unit of learning and assessment leading to the award of credit. A group of selected modules will normally lead to a designated qualification ... the existence of modular qualifications in vocational education is already widespread. The size and definitions of modules vary, however, between the different awarding bodies ... Modules only have a logic in terms of the broader qualifications and set of awards of which they form a part.*

Postlethwait (1985, p. 3398):

> *No definition of a* module *has been acceptable to everyone, and as a consequence, the term has been applied variously to include all sorts of units, materials, and the combination. However, in each case a module seems to represent a self-contained instructional package covering a single conceptual unit of subject matter.*

Reuling & Sauter (1996, p. 5):

> *In vocational education and training,* modules *are part-qualifications which are taught, assessed and credited separately. The frameworks for such a dismantling of qualification clusters are overall qualifications within the horizontal and vertical structure of a qualification system.*
> [In der Berufsausbildung werden unter Modulen Teilqualifikationen verstanden, die separat vermittelt, geprüft und zertifiziert werden. Der Bezugsrahmen für eine solche Zerlegung von Qualifikationsbündeln sind Gesamtqualifikationen innerhalb einer horizontalen und vertikalen Qualifikationsstruktur.]

Schmidt (1997a, p. 3):

> *The origin of the term* 'module' *in the areas of work organisation and technology refers to a 'part of a whole', to a component and – in vocational education and training – to a phase of training and education. However, there was and is no generally accepted definition which would have clearly separated the term from other concepts.*
> [Die Herkunft des Begriffs 'Modul' aus dem arbeitsorganisatorisch-technischen Bereich verweist auf einen 'Teil des Ganzen', einen 'Baustein' und – in der Berufsbildung – auf einen Ausbildungsabschnitt. Eine allgemein akzeptierte Definition des Begriffes, die seine Verwendung trennscharf von anderen Termine abgehoben hätte, gab es und gibt es allerdings nicht.]

Schmidt (1997b, p. 42):

> Modules *in vocational education and training are phases in initial and further training which refer didactically to contexts of knowledge and activity. They are concluded with an assessment in the form of a certificate. If they are combined like building blocks they can form an overall qualification.*
> [Module in der beruflichen Bildung sind didaktisch auf einen Kenntnis- und Tätigkeitszusammenhang bezogene Aus- und Weiterbildungsabschnitte mit einem bewerteten Abschluß in Form eines Zeugnisses. Sie können wie Bausteine zu einer Gesamtqualifikation zusammengesetzt werden.]

Sellin (1994b, p. 2):

> *The term* module *refers to part of a building, a system or product and is originally a technical term. A system is composed of a multitude of modules or elements each of which is in itself indispensable and contributes to the operation of the entire system. In the world of occupational educational science the term module is both an organizational principle and a didactic or methodological principle ...*

Sloane (1997a, p. 225):

> *From a technical point of view,* 'modules' *are prefabricated parts which are used in bigger entities. What matters is the relationship between the part and the whole, in which the module as a part is a whole itself. This wholeness of a module is to be embedded into a 'bigger' whole.*
> ['Module' sind in einer eher technischen Betrachtung vorgefertigte funktionsfähige Teile, die in einer größeren Einheit Verwendung finden. Es geht um das Verhältnis von Teil und Ganzes, wobei das Modul als Teil selbst ein Ganzes

ist. Diese Ganzheit Modul soll in ein 'größeres' Ganzes eingebettet werden.]

Theodossin (1986, p. 9):

we may define modules *as: A measured part (or course) of an extended learning experience leading to the attainment of a specified qualification(s), for which a designated number (and, possibly, sequence) of modules is required, with the group of designated/required modules known as a programme, a programme of studies, or a modular-course structure.*

Wiegand (1996b, p. 28):

By modules, *we mean short-term educational/training units or blocs which are complete in themselves and examinable as such.*

Young (1995, p. 171):

I shall define modularization *as the breaking up of the curriculum into discrete and relatively short learning experiences.*

APPENDIX III. Characteristics of Modules in VET

In this appendix, the characteristics of modules in VET, as presented in chapter 3, are to be derived from a technical example. This method of induction seems to be appropriate as the term 'module' itself originates from technical contexts. Postlethwait (1985) derives the definition of modules in education from the use of the term in biology, and Kloas (1997b) illustrates his definition of modules with the relationship of the elements of a building (= modules) and the building as a whole. In this appendix, the use of modules or components in the motor manufacturing industry should clarify the application of modules in VET. The subheadings of Table III in chapter 3 are used.

Integrative Function

The individual components of a vehicle, like wheels, the rear-view mirror, the heating system, the engine, the clutch, etc. contribute to the overall function 'driving'. The combination of the elements not only represents the sum of their part-functions but also generates additionally the overall function.

In VET, the overall function may be defined as the 'ability of the individual to act and work competently in an occupational environment (vocational competence)', as developed in chapters 2 and 3. The functions of modules in VET are integrated into this overall function. The sum of the individual modules constitutes the qualification's overall function.

This integrative function does not exclude modules that have an independent function. A car radio or a child's safety seat in a vehicle adds the functions 'listening to music' and 'safe transportation of a child' to the car's genuine function of 'driving' (see *additional competences*). In the right conditions, these components are also reasonably usable outside the vehicle.

In the training sector, some modules may also be utilised independently from the genuine overall function. If modules like a driving licence for a forklift truck or fluency in a foreign language are part of a qualification, they provide additional functions, but they cannot substitute the overall function of a qualification. Their independent usability often gives these modules a special status within the overall qualification.

Standard Definition

Some components (wheels, braking system and engine) are indispensable for the basic function of a vehicle. Driving without one of these modules is not possible. Other components (airbag, anti-lock braking system, air-conditioning system, and shock absorber) contribute to the wishes of discriminating customers for safe and convenient driving.

In VET, there are also differences between the minimal requirements of a qualification and the preparation of individuals for higher levels of employment. The standards of different levels of qualifications are dependent on the stage of development of an economy and society. In the context of the Western European countries, the preparation for simple manual and executing work (European level one) [138] is increasingly regarded as an insufficient qualification for the vast majority of people. The overall function of a qualification ('vocational competence') requires increasingly the acquisition of sophisticated vocational skills.

Outcome Orientation

For the use of a vehicle, it is not important how its components are produced. The production process of the parts is of no significance as long as their quality and fit (described by technical standards) are ensured.

If – as derived from the technical context – modules in VET contribute to the overall function of the qualification, their quality will be measured by their benefit for the overall function. Following this argument, it is insignificant which teaching methods and styles (group work/whole class teaching, formal/informal teaching) or learning situations (school-/work-based training, subject/cross-subject learning) are used. Decisive is the contribution of the module to the overall function of the qualification, not the process by which this contribution is achieved. Therefore, modules represent categories of outcome or competence.

Restricted Variability

The example of the construction of a vehicle illustrates very clearly that the order in which components are fitted together to form a whole is not completely variable. Before the engine, the seats, the windscreen, etc. can be installed, the major parts of the bodywork have to be fitted together. However, the three components mentioned can be installed in various orders, as soon as the bodywork is completed.

Transferred to education and training, the variability of the temporal sequence in which modules are ordered is restricted by pedagogic criteria. The content of bookkeeping requires certain mathematical skills as a basis; other skills can be learnt in variable order. The level of restrictions in the temporal sequence of modules in VET may vary from one occupation to another.

Accepted Standards

Following the argumentation in the previous sections, all modules contribute to the overall function of the whole and the combination of modules is restricted by required temporal sequences and dependent on aspects of content. Therefore, accepted norms and standards are required to ensure the comparability and intelligibility of modules. The standards are conditional upon combining modules.

In the technical contexts, some of these accepted standards have a long tradition and are widely used (e.g. German Industrial Standards – *Deutsche Industrienormen [DIN]*); in many cases they are even a precondition for the marketability of products (e.g. strict quality standards for the products of motor manufacturing industries' suppliers). In the wake of total quality management (TQM), these aspects of standardised and comparable product qualities are increasingly influential.

In VET, the recognition of modularised qualifications is dependent on the degree to which the standards of the individual modules are accepted. Furthermore, modules can only contribute to the overall function of the qualification, and modules of different providers can only be combined, if accepted standards ensure their intelligibility. Accepted standards also contribute to clear entrance requirements to courses and to permeability in the overall educational system.

General Standards

Standards for modules not only determine the content of modules but also their reach. In the example given, standards for components could only be valid for one vehicle or one series of vehicles. In practice, most companies have standards for all of their cars; and safety standards are often binding for all cars to be sold in a country. In this context, the term 'module' is only used if the standards of component are relevant to more than one type of car. Striving for economies of scale in the production process pushes the development of widely accepted standards ahead.

In the training sector, there are also standards with a different reach (valid for a single provider, all providers of a region, national standards, EU standards). There is no agreement on the reach required for a 'module' to be so defined. Most commentators argue that provisions that are only valid for one company or one provider are not modules even if they are termed as such. We can speak of 'modules' only if the regulating standards are relevant for more than one or a few companies and providers of qualifications. The possibilities of increased efficiency achieved by widely applicable (or general) standards for modules in VET seem to be far from exhausted. For the trainee, the value of qualification is highest if it is recognised and, therefore, marketable nationwide, Europe- or even worldwide. To ensure the flexibility of a modular system, this entails, therefore, that modules in VET should be recognised at these levels as well.

Multiple Relevance

Closely linked with general standards is the question of the relevance of modules. The suppliers of the motor manufacturing industry aim to produce components that can be used in more than one type of vehicle. Car radios, headrests, air-conditioning systems, etc. can be used with only insignificant adaptations in cars, vans and heavy goods vehicles.

In VET, this sharing of modules means that they are relevant to more than one occupation. Certain basic skills like welding, soldering, and sanding are relevant to many occupations in the wide range of metalworking industries. It is characteristic for such multi-relevant modules that they contribute to the overall function of several qualifications if the modules' standards ensure their fit. Again, comparable to the technical context, the use of these modules enhances the efficiency of provisions.

Additional Competences

Additional competences, acquired in initial training and/or further education, can improve the learner's position in an increasingly competitive environment. Just as additional components of a vehicle improve its usability (a roof rack or a tow bar improve the function 'transport'), additional modules in VET (foreign language or information technology skills, skills related to other occupational areas, etc.) can extend the degree to which an employee is able to adapt to new demands of the world of work. A precondition for the improvement of competences by additional modules is the reasonable combination of the modules.

Individual Modification

The standards and design of components of vehicles are changeable without changing the vehicle as a whole. The improvement of the braking system or of impact absorbers may be necessary as a reaction to tightened safety standards. No manufacturer would design a completely new vehicle only to fulfil the new standards.

Transferred to VET, this characteristic of modularisation can enhance the possibilities of reacting to increasingly rapidly changing production processes and modes of communication in the world of work. The reaction in the training sector can take place quicker and cheaper if it is not necessary to replace a whole qualification but only to modify or renew certain modules.

APPENDIX IV. Modularisation in Selected Countries of the EU [139]

Spain

In Spain [140], the 1990 education reform act, LOGSE (*Ley Orgánica de Ordinación Géneral del Sistema Educativo*), introduced modular concepts to restructure the educational system. Due to the disappearance of the traditional apprenticeship system in the 1960s and the low status of vocational compared to academic higher education, the main objectives of the modular concepts were to overcome the academic/vocational divide in education and to lay stronger emphasis on the sector of initial training than hitherto. As a consequence of the formal equality of general and vocational education, vocational contents are compulsory parts of general secondary schools and certain modularised vocational qualifications give the right to university entrance. Furthermore, continuing training (*formación profesional Ocupational*) provides routes into higher education for working people.

Initial vocational education and training (*formación profesional Reglada*) takes place almost exclusively in schools but includes obligatory periods of practical instruction. The qualifications are not organised in school years but in curricular entities, comprising up to 1200 hours of instruction. These modules are self-contained part-qualifications and consist of a foundation and a specialised level, with the foundation level being compulsory at secondary school. The specialised level comprises the post-compulsory sector of initial training and is divided into two levels:

- *module 2:* middle-level modules, corresponding to category 2 in the 1985 EU stage system for vocational qualifications; and
- *module 3:* higher-level modules, corresponding to category 3 in the EU stage system of vocational qualifications.

To increase the marketability of the modules, they can also be combined to lead to an integrated professional qualification. In this case, individual modules can be part of several qualifications and can be combined freely, restricted only by the marketability of the overall qualification.

Characteristically, curricula and modules are designed on a regional rather than a central level. Employers and trade unions are involved in this process. The potential of modularised systems to take local and regional needs into account more than traditional systems seems to be increasingly important considering the drive within the EU for a 'Europe of the Regions'.

As the Spanish example shows, modularisation can assume the function of an overall integrative framework in the case that the whole education sector is reformed (Cleve & Kell, 1996, p. 19). In Spain, modules not only regulate the transfer from compulsory school to the world of work but also the transition from initial and continuing training to higher education.

France

In France [141], disadvantaged or unemployed juveniles are trained in modular structures (adults are not normally entitled to take part). The first aim of the CFI-modules (*Crédit Formation Individualisée*), composed of about 40 hours, is to give the trainees confidence in their abilities. In a sequence of steps, the participants are then enabled to take part in regular training, which leads to recognised qualifications – in most cases to the CAP certificate (*Certificat d'Aptitude Professionnelle*). Initial tests are conducted to assess potentials and weaknesses as well as prior learning experiences of trainees. Based on the test results, the appropriate entrance level is identified. The programme comprises three main stages, which also serve as possible entrance levels:

- *level 1:* remedial measures to catch up with weaknesses in basic skills;
- *level 2:* vocational preparation; and
- *level 3:* vocational qualification.

The levels must be seen in the wider context of the organisation of French education in stages at compulsory schools and at institutions of higher education. Within these levels, the modules are combined into clusters to avoid the danger of a lack of cohesion between the modules.

The clusters represent part-qualifications in the system of *Unités Capitalisables* (UC), a modularised framework of certificates assigned to the level below that of 'skilled worker' in the French hierarchy of vocational qualifications.[142] The manageable size and the flexibility of the modules allow for individual learning problems to be taken into account much more effectively than in traditional systems. Success with the comparatively small modules provides valuable reassurance for the often insecure trainees. Moreover, the emphasis on the principle of 'learning to learn' highlights the responsiveness of the programme to individual learning needs. Individual modules are in general not marketable; their value lies in the preparation for a regular qualification.

The modular structures are, therefore, primarily used to regulate the sector of vocational preparation of particular target groups. Whilst widely employed in continuing training, modules are rarely found in regular initial training, which is in general almost exclusively provided by the school sector. Therefore, modular structures can be regarded as closing the gap between initial training and sectors of vocational preparation and continuing training (Manning, 1996, p. 308).

Netherlands

In the Netherlands [143], modular structures in vocational education and training are the result of gradual reforms in the 1980s, which were intended to introduce market forces to the sector. Since then, employers and trade unions have been the dominant players in the regulation of training. Consequently, there are substantial differences in the type of training provision found between the economic sectors. For example, modularised systems can be found in the retail trade, the installation and plumbing sector, the printing industry and in most new occupational fields like logistics and computerisation.[144] In these sector-specific provisions there are substantially different concepts of modularisation in practice. Because of its contribution to the reform debate in Germany, the far-reaching approach in the printing sector will be explained in some detail.

In 1993, the existing system of training in the printing industry was modularised, with the aim of increasing the flexibility of provisions and to integrate initial and continuing training. As a spin-off, new forms of cooperation between vocational schools and work-based training provisions were developed. Modules are offered in four fields [145]:

- general certificates (e.g. languages, science, technology);
- certificates in six occupational areas (design, management, print preparation, printing, quality control, packing);
- vocational certificates (e.g. administration, marketing, production for the occupational area of management) (22 modules to chose from); and

- specialised certificates (e.g. purchase, sale, advertising for the vocational area of marketing) (67 modules).

Eight modules from these fields form a vocational qualification; single modules are not marketable. Five of the modules must be chosen from 'general certificates', a regulation which mirrors the strong emphasis laid on theory and general educational content in Dutch vocational qualifications since the 1960s. Of the remaining three modules, one has to be chosen from each of the other fields. Whereas the courses in the six 'occupational areas' are to provide a broad vocational knowledge base, the highly modularised 'specialised certificates' are to increase the flexibility of the qualification. Short-term responses to changing market situations and individual retraining later in the career are possible by choosing a different module or additional 'specialised modules'. The order in which the eight modules are taken, assessed and credited is flexible; there are no final examinations. The GOC (*Grafisch Opleidingscentrum*), as the national educational institution for the graphic industry – ruled by the social partners and educationists – is responsible for the quality and the curriculum of the qualification.

This highly flexible framework allows the accreditation of prior learning (e.g. certain 'general certificates' may be credited for trainees with higher school certificates) and the individual duration of the overall qualification can range from between 1½ and 4 years.

Scotland

In Scotland [146], all non-advanced vocational courses for post-compulsory students were reformed during the period 1983–85.[147] After the reform, over 3000 modules covered all occupational areas. Under the responsibility of the Scottish Vocational Education Council (SCOTVEC), modules are accredited through the National Certificate (NC), which provides a single cohesive framework. Overcoming the confusing range of vocational certificates of pre-reform times was one of the main aims of modularisation.

NC modules are defined in learning outcomes, i.e. what is to be learned, assessed and certificated is described by the knowledge, skills and behaviour trainees should be able to display at the end of the module, not by the process of teaching. The modules of about 40 hours are self-sufficient units. Until 1990, SCOTVEC did not accredit combinations of modules, although typical study programmes were clustered to meet the requirements of specific occupational areas. The introduction of Scottish Vocational Qualifications (SVQs) in 1990 and of General Scottish Vocational Qualifications (GSVQs) in 1992 marks a move away from individual awards (*individual modules*) to group awards (combination of *programme modules*) (Stanyer, 1997, p. 55). Parallel to these developments, industry gained influence on the content of the modules and now has the responsibility for setting standards of competence for SVQs. Thus, three groups of modules can be identified:

- *NC modules:* existent for all economic sectors, credited as free-standing units, providing vocational preparation and orientation;
- *GSVQs:* based on NC modules, awarded as a combination of modules, providing a broad foundation in a vocational area on three levels; and
- *SVQs:* based on NC modules, GSVQs or specifically designed modules, awarded as a combination of modules, providing basic and specific competences in one particular occupational sector.

Similar to Spain, modularisation in Scotland was used to reform the entire sector of vocational education and training. In this 'system focus' (Bruijn & Howieson, 1995, p. 90), modules are not defined in relation to specific occupations but can be used for a variety of qualifications. The process of modularisation started with the design of modules that were then built up into courses and qualifications (e.g. group awards like SVQs and GSVQs). The enormous number of modules is the consequence of this process.

The Dutch process of modularisation is distinctly different from the Scottish: it started from breaking down existing courses into modules. In this 'skill focus', modules refer to competences relevant for specific occupational areas. The sector-specific training system in the Netherlands has a beneficial effect on this approach. The strategy of modularisation in the context of Germany, as suggested in chapter 6, follows the 'skill focus'.

The challenge of creating a cohesive and flexible framework, responsive to changing skill needs and individual preferences, can be met by both approaches towards modular structures as long as they take national and regional conditions of the economic system into account.[148]

APPENDIX V.
Definition of the European Dimension in Education [149]

The purpose of this resolution is to strengthen the European dimension in education by launching a series of concerted measures for the period 1988–92; these measures could help to:

- strengthen in young people a sense of European identity and make clear to them the value of European civilisation and of the foundations on which the European peoples intend to base their development today, that is, in particular the safeguarding of the principles of democracy, social justice and respect for human rights (Copenhagen declaration, April 1978);
- prepare young people to take part in the economic and social development of the Community and in making concrete progress towards European union as stipulated in the Single European Act;

- make them aware of the advantages which the Community represents, but also of the challenges it involves, in opening up an enlarged economic and social area to them;
- improve their knowledge of the Community and its member states in their historical, cultural, economic and social aspects and bring home to them the significance of the cooperation of the member states of the European Community with other countries of Europe and the world.

APPENDIX VI. Definitions of NVQ and GNVQ Levels

Level 1

Competence which involves the application of knowledge in the performance of a range of varied work activities, most of which may be routine and predictable.

Level 2

Competence which involves the application of knowledge in a significant range of varied work activities, performed in a variety of contexts. Some of the activities are complex or non-routine, and there is some individual responsibility or autonomy. Collaboration with others, perhaps through membership of a work group or team, may often be a requirement.

Level 3

Competence which involves the application of knowledge in a broad range of varied work activities performed in a wide variety of contexts and most of which are complex and non-routine. There is considerable responsibility and autonomy, and control or guidance of others is often required.

Level 4

Competence which involves the application of knowledge in a broad range of complex, technical or professional work activities performed in a wide variety of contexts and with a substantial degree of personal responsibility and autonomy. Responsibility for the work of others and the allocation of resources is often present.

Level 5

Competence which involves the application of a significant range of fundamental principles across a wide and often unpredictable variety of contexts. Very substantial personal autonomy, and often significant responsibility for the work of others and for the allocation of substantial resources feature strongly, as do personal accountabilities for analysis and diagnosis, design, planning, execution and evaluation.

Table AI. NVQ levels.[150]

Level of award	Entry requirements	Number of mandatory vocational units	Number of optional vocational units	Number of mandatory core skill units	Regular duration of courses (in years)	Equivalent qualifications
Advanced	4 to 5 GCSEs (grades A–C), or Intermediate GNVQ	8	4	3 (at level 3)	2	NVQ level 3 Two A levels BTEC National Certificates and Diplomas
Intermediate	1 to 2 GCSEs (grades A–D), or Foundation GNVQ	4	2	3 (at level 2)	1	NVQ level 2 Four to five GCSEs (grades A*–C) BTEC First Certificates and Diplomas
Foundation	No access requirements	3	3	3 (at level 1)	1	NVQ level 1 Four GCSEs (grades D–F)

Table AII. GNVQ levels: requirements and equivalent qualifications.[151]

Notes

1. Mandatory vocational units at all levels and optional vocational units at the advanced and intermediate level must be drawn from the same vocational area. Optional vocational units at the foundation level can be drawn from different vocational areas.
2. Core skill units are mandatory in Communication, Application of Number and Information Technology. Additional core skill units can be awarded in Working with Others, Problem Solving and Learning and Performance.
3. Students are encouraged to gain additional units to increase the scope and range of their GNVQ. Additional units may be further core skills or vocational units from other GNVQs or from NVQs. Elements of GCSEs or A/AS levels are also possible.
4. It is possible for students to finish earlier or later than the regular duration of courses indicate.
5. As there are no formal entry requirements, the details given here only indicate informal guidelines.

APPENDIX VII. Unit of Competence from NVQ *Health Care Support* [152]

Unit:

Assist the client to achieve emotional comfort and rest

Element 1: ***Assist in minimising client discomfort and pain***

Performance criteria:

- the client is encouraged to express feelings of discomfort or pain, and is encouraged to use self-help methods to control these in accordance with the plan of care
- information agreed with the care team about pain or discomfort and ways in which it can be minimised, is given in a manner, and at a level and pace, appropriate to the client
- the client is assisted to maintain a comfortable position consistent with the plan of care and as agreed with the car team
- the client's condition is monitored in accordance with the plan of care
- requests form the client to minimise pain, or changes in the client's condition, are reported immediately to the appropriate member(s) of the care team and recorded accurately, legibly and completely in the appropriate document
- other clients disturbed by the client's pain are given reassurance, as and when necessary

Range: Clients groups: all
Care settings: all
All types of pain and discomfort

Element 2: ***Assist in providing conditions to meet the client's need for rest***

Performance criteria:

- the client is assisted to prepare and place him/herself in a position which is comfortable, is conductive to rest and is consistent with the plan of care
- as agreed with the care team and in accordance with organisational policy and practice, the client is assisted to take any prescribe medication as part of preparation for rest consistent with the plan of care
- the client is comforted, offered reassurance and encouraged to rest, through verbal and/or non verbal means
- the client is monitored according to the plan of care and unusual circumstances are reported and/or recorded accurately
- the job-holder's own movements and behaviour are modified to assist the client's rest
- others entering the environment are reminded of the need to modify their behaviour and/or movements, if necessary
- adjustments are made to heating, ventilation, noise and light of environment to facilitate sleep rest as far as is possible

Range: Client groups: all
Care settings: all

Element 3: ***Contribute to the prevention and management of client distress***

Performance criteria:

- where possible, client's belongings are placed according to his/her preferences
- behaviour which has previously indicated distress, or changes in the client's condition, are brought to the attention of the appropriate member of the care team with minim possible delay
- when the client appears to be becoming distressed, immediate reassurance is given by verbal or non-verbal means and consistent with any client beliefs
- where feelings of fear or aggression are expressed, these are treated in a manner which acknowledges the expression as meaningful and important to the client
- the client is given sufficient time, space and privacy to express their distress
- in all cases where the job-holder is unsure of their ability to calm the patient or of the effects that distress my have on the client's condition, appropriate assistance from other care team members is requested

Range: Client groups: all and relation to all personal, cultural and religious beliefs
Care settings: all
Care team: job-holder, professional staff, other supervisors, client, relatives, friends
Information: is that which is agreed with the care team

Figure A3.

APPENDIX VIII. Unit from GNVQ Intermediate *Health & Social Care* [153]

Unit:

Inter-personal relati-onships

Element 1: ...

Performance criteria:
1. ...
2. ...
3. ...

Range:
- ...
- ...

...

Evidence indicators:

...

Amplification and guidance:
- Performance criterion 1:

...
- Performance criterion ...:

...
- ...

Element 2: ***Explore how interpersonal relationships may be affected by discriminatory behaviour***

Performance criteria:
1. provide examples of the different forms which **discrimination** may take
2. describe **behaviours** which may indicate discrimination
3. describe how stereotyping individuals and groups can lead to discriminatory behaviour
4. describe the possible **effects** of discrimination
5. identify the **rights** which all individuals have under current equality of opportunity legislation

Range:
- Discrimination based on: age, disability, gender, health status, race, religion, sexuality
- Behaviours: direct, indirect
- Effects: short-term, long-term
- Rights under the following legislation: Sex Discrimination Acts 1975 and 1986, Race Relation Act 1976, The Chronically Sick and Disabled Act 1986, Equal Pay Act 1970 (amended 1988), Fair Employment Act 1989

Evidence indicators:
A report which conveys the meaning of the term 'discrimination' by giving examples of four different bases of discrimination. The report should describe the behaviours which may indicate discrimination, how different groups can be stereotyped and the possible long-term and short-term effects of discrimination The report should also identify the equality of opportunity rights which individuals have under current legislation.

Amplification and guidance:
- Performance criterion 2:

Direct behaviours would include abusive language, overt behaviour, not touching those believed to be infected, racist/sexist jokes, talking to someone pushing the wheelchair rather than the occupant. Indirect behaviour includes such areas as tone of voice, body language, avoidance, not providing advice or support to elderly people in relation to sexual activity.
- Performance criterion 4:

Short-term effects include anger, loss of feeling of self-worth; long-term effects include detrimental employment prospects, lack of motivation.

Element 3: ...
Performance criteria: ...
Range: ...
Evidence indicators: ...
Amplification and guidance: ...

Element ...

Figure A4.